C0-AQA-955

Within My Grasp

This book is dedicated to my wife, Mary Ann, for her support and patience throughout the years; to all amputees and their families in hopes that they will find the strength to overcome their obstacles and live their lives to the fullest degree possible by believing that they can do it; and to my good friend and fellow pilot Jeff Sharman, who left us too soon.

Mike Penketh
with Marti Smiley Childs
and Jeff March

EDITPROS℠

Published by EditPros LLC
423 F Street, suite 206
Davis, CA 95616
www.editpros.com

Copyright © 2013 by EditPros LLC
First edition
This book is copyright under the Berne Convention.
All rights reserved. No reproduction without permission.
The EditPros logo is a federally registered service mark
of EditPros LLC.

ISBN-10: 1937317099
ISBN-13: 978-1-937317-096
Library of Congress Control Number: 2013933809
Printed in the United States of America

CATALOGING INFORMATION:
Penketh, Mike, Childs, Marti Smiley, and March, Jeff
        Within My Grasp
    Filing categories:
        Autobiography
        Biography

Cover photo (black & white 1988) by Jeff March;
Cover design by Erin Michele Childs

Contents

Foreword

What would you do if you found yourself awakening from a deep slumber to discover that your hands were missing? How would you eat, or drink? How would you brush your teeth? How would you change your clothes? How would you turn a doorknob? How would you answer the phone? How would you sign a check, or fill out a form? The frustrations are endless, but survival is a human instinct, so you would have to figure out how to do things, or have someone do everything for you. The innate instinct for survival can get you by, but the human spirit and a strong sense of pride can help you overcome obstacles at a much faster pace.

Loss of arms (upper-limb amputation) is far less common than loss of legs (lower-limb amputation).

V

Physical medicine and rehabilitation expert Dr. Timothy R. Dillingham and his colleagues at Johns Hopkins University investigated trends in amputation rates in the United States and published their findings in the *Southern Medical Journal*, volume 95 (pages 875–883) in 2002. Using hospital discharge data from 1988 to 1996, their research showed that the number of lower-limb losses was more than six times greater than the total of upper-limb losses during those eight years. Lower-limb loss tends to result from vascular problems—impaired blood circulation—whereas most upper-limb loss is due to trauma—as it was in Mike Penketh's case. Of the more than 1 million amputations that occurred during the study period, only two-tenths of 1 percent (a total of 462) were bilateral upper-limb losses—those in which patients lost part or all of both arms. Because of that low percentage, as well as the fine motor functions performed by hands, technology to assist upper-limb amputees has lagged behind lower-limb assistive devices, primarily due to economics.

More recent statistics appear in a Congressional Research Services report, dated February 5, 2013, by Hannah Fischer. The report shows a substantial increase in amputations between September 2001 and December 2012, according to the Army Office of the Surgeon General records. This increase is a result of U.S. military casualties in Operation New Dawn (OND), Operation Iraqi Freedom (OIF) and Operation Enduring Freedom (OEF). As of December 3, 2012, a total of 1,715 amputations occurred during OND, OIF, and OEF conflicts. The total includes 1,493 major limb amputations and 222 minor amputations. More than half of the total amputations resulted from improvised explosive devices.

Another disturbing statistic is the number of traumatic brain injuries sustained from OIF and OEM. A Department of Defense report titled, "Report to Congress in Accordance with Section 1634 (b) of the National Defense Authorization Act for Fiscal Year 2008," the Military Health System recorded 43,779 patients diagnosed with traumatic brain injury in calendar years 2003 through 2007. Along with his amputations, Mike sustained traumatic brain injury, making his recovery even more difficult.

"You work with what you have," says Mike, a bilateral amputee. "And you never give up on your dreams."

Within a remarkably short time of losing his hands,

Mike became determined to resume flying airplanes. He was fitted for and tried numerous hook devices and prosthetic arms before his relentless pursuit led him to a technologically advanced solution that performed some critical hand functions. Then he fought for two years with the Federal Aviation Administration (FAA) to regain his pilot's license, and went on to fly in aerobatics shows to prove to himself and to the naysayers that he could do it.

An inspiration to school children, Mike travels to Northern California grade schools as part of the non-profit Touch of Understanding program. His mission is to teach young children, teachers and parents to respect and have empathy for all individuals. The program encourages its participants to focus on their own strengths rather than on weaknesses, and to realize that everyone faces adversity and frustrations—some visible, others concealed—that they may struggle to overcome.

While Mike captivates the attention of kids with his motorized hands, he never misses a chance to give a little pep talk about overcoming obstacles. He quizzes them, "How does a marathon runner run a marathon? By simply starting with the first step. How does a student do a homework assignment? By simply starting with the first page. I chose to start a new life, one step at a time," Mike tells them.

"Touch of Understanding has been a great program for me. The process of explaining how I cope with my disability has given me a lot of confidence in myself. I got into it because I wanted something out of it, but as it turns out I've been able to pass my message to a lot of young people," he said.

"I've learned to appreciate people. I've become very patient even though I wasn't before. I once was the kind of guy who said I don't care—if it's in my way, I'll just step on it and keep on marching. There were no bumps in the road. Now, there are a lot of bumps in the road that I've learned to work around. I've also learned to let people help me work around those bumps."

Within My Grasp

X

Chapter 1

Extensively Devitalized in Utah

I didn't know where I was, and I didn't know the guy who was leaning over me. I had been unconscious, and I was flat on my back, but as I began awakening in a groggy, dull fog, I sensed that I was in some kind of aircraft. Over the engine noise, the pilot spoke.

"We have a Level 1 AirMed patient aboard, and we're about five miles out. Prepare for severe limb damage, possible head injury. The patient is male, in his 40s." The pilot was contacting the radio dispatch room at the University of Utah Hospital Trauma Services Unit in Salt Lake City. I did not comprehend that I was the patient. Everything revolved in slow motion around me. I felt cold, numb. And then I blacked out again.

It was September 22, 1993. I had been in a horrific, grinding crash, about which I have no recollection. They told me that rescue workers took about 30 minutes to peel the wreckage apart and extricate me, before I was loaded onto a medevac helicopter and flown to the University of Utah Medical Center. I don't remember landing at the hospital or being whisked through the corridors on a gurney, but I must have been a gruesomely bloody, bandaged mess. The emergency responders wheeled me straight into the hospital's emergency room. I was weak, pale and semiconscious. Gowned physicians and other medical personnel swarmed around me. They began assessing my condition. As I began coming to again, I wanted to ask where I was and what they were doing to me, but I was unable to speak.

A nurse hurriedly wrapped a blood pressure cuff around my right upper arm and hooked it up to a monitor. I couldn't understand why they seemed so frantic, or why I couldn't move or feel much of anything. I had no idea that both of my forearms had been shredded. A physician, who shined a small light into my eyes to gauge my reflexes, shouted, *"What are his vitals?"*

My blood pressure was soaring. *"BP 190 over 130; pulse 95; respiration 16 and shallow, temperature 97 degrees,"* the nurse responded.

Another physician blurted, *"He's lost a lot of blood! The patient has a right periorbital hematoma, but his pupils are equally round and reactive and globes are intact. The patient has no pulses in his distal right upper extremity, and he has no distal left upper extremity."*

"Distal right upper extremity." That meant the end of my right arm—my hand. I had no pulse in my right hand. And "no distal left extremity." In clinical terms, the physician catalogued the grotesque injuries to my extremities. *"There's partial amputation of the left hand with a large amount of soft tissue disruption and bony misalignment of the hand. The right forearm shows a gross amount of soft tissue swelling and extensive trauma to the soft tissues of the wrist and hand."*

I was confused and unable to offer doctors any information about the accident that I had been in. Doctors wanted to know about my medical history, but I managed to convey only two vital pieces of information: that I'm allergic to penicillin, and that I have high blood pressure. Despite the severity of my injuries, I felt more numbness than pain. And I couldn't seem to catch my breath. I should have been terrified, but in my deep confusion, I was merely curious about my surroundings. The triage physicians quickly took steps to stabilize my condition and reinforce my weak, irregular breathing.

"The patient will require resuscitation with two IVs," a physician declared. *"He needs the standard trauma X-rays and lab evaluations. He also needs intubation to control his variable respiratory effort."*

As I lay on the examination table, a technician used a portable X-ray machine to record images to evaluate the condition of my spine. Even while the X-rays were being taken, doctors continued issuing medical orders. *"He needs head and abdominal CT scans. If those are normal, he can go to the OR for repair of his upper extremities."*

Diagnostic lab and X-ray reports came back promptly and revealed at least some good news: my chest X-ray and lateral spine images were normal. My overall condition was deteriorating, though, and I needed medications quickly. By then the anesthesiologist had arrived to prepare me for surgery. Intravenous needles normally are inserted into hands or forearms. I didn't understand it then, but one of my hands was nearly completely gone, and both of my arms were too mangled to be useful. So the anesthesiologist improvised and penetrated a blood vessel in my collarbone area. I guess it must have hurt, but I don't remember. And I still didn't know what I was doing there or where all that blood was coming from.

After I was wheeled into the operating room, neurosurgeons went to work. Because of the likelihood that I had a brain injury and the possibility that my brain would start swelling dangerously, they prepared to insert a pressure monitoring device to evaluate my brain functions.

"We're going to place an ICP bolt in the right frontal calvarium to monitor intracranial pressure," someone said as a second team of surgeons prepared to begin work on my mutilated arms. A nurse shaved the top of my head. I wondered what that was about, but couldn't seem to form the words to ask. I felt something pulling on my scalp. And then I heard a drill. The neurosurgeons were boring a hole into my skull. I learned later that they inserted a hollow bolt and fed a catheter through the hole to monitor pressure inside my skull and to expel any buildup of cerebral spinal fluid. And I still had no idea about what had happened.

Mary Ann—who is now my wife but was my girlfriend at the time—was at our home in the Northern

California town of Vacaville when she received a call from a physician at the University of Utah Medical Center. He told her that I had been in a serious accident. Mary Ann asked, "Is he going to make it?" The doctor hesitated before replying, "He has a pretty good chance." He told her that all of the fingers on one of my hands had been scraped off. Mary Ann said her first thought was, "Oh my God, he's never going to fly again." She knew that flying almost entirely defined who I was. I was a pilot, an adventurer, first and foremost. Just about everything else took a back seat. The physician told her, "He's in surgery, and you need to come as soon as possible."

Although the surgeons had hoped to repair damage, their examination revealed far greater injuries than the initial emergency room examination showed. Much of my left hand had been ground off in the crash.

Mary Ann immediately began making airline reservations and other preparations—finding someone to take care of our house and animals, and letting close friends and relatives know about the accident. In the midst of all that, Mary Ann received another call as she was preparing to depart about two hours later. It was the same physician from University of Utah, and he said that he was sorry that what remained of my left hand was too far mangled to save. The doctor told her that surgeons had performed an amputation at my left wrist. I can't imagine the horror and sense of helplessness that she must have felt at that moment.

My right forearm was almost completely severed, and I had irreparable muscle and blood vessel damage. Still, the surgeons initially hoped to salvage my right arm and hand, if possible. I was moved into the intensive-care unit, where I spent the night. By morning, pressure caused by my mauling injuries had begun to interfere with blood circulation, as documented in the medical report: *"There was extensively devitalized forearm musculature to the approximate one-third of the forearm."* Extensively devitalized; a medical term that means no longer functioning. The report continued, *"There was an avulsion injury of the palmar and thenar musculature, and thrombosis of the radial and ulnar arteries."* The muscles of my right palm and thumb had been torn away, and two major arteries in my lower arm had been crushed. *Overall, this was deemed non-salvageable for reimplantation, and completion of the amputation was then accomplished."* The grinding crash that I had survived had pulverized complex bone structures as well as delicate nerves, muscles and ligaments, leaving only shredded, bloodied tissue behind. The enormity of the damage dictated their only course of action. The surgeons amputated my mutilated right arm about four inches below my elbow.

Our friend and neighbor Sheila Sharman insisted on flying to Salt Lake City with Mary Ann. They arrived in Utah early the next morning, while I was in surgery to amputate my right arm. She was greeted with more bad news. A neurosurgeon came into the waiting room and said to Mary Ann, "Mike has a very severe head injury." He continued, "After a year you should have a pretty good idea of how he's going to be." He described my head injury as similar to taking a bowl of Jell-O and shaking it up just before it hardens. It develops lots of cracks. He said, "That's how Mike's brain is."

Mary Ann said she barely recognized me when they brought me out of surgery. My face was swollen, and my head was about twice its normal size. She saw the probe that the neurosurgeons had inserted into the top of my head to relieve the pressure. My arms were thickly bandaged.

After the amputation surgeries, the anesthesiologist kept me on an intravenous drug that induced a state of semi-consciousness, and I remained that way for about 10 days. I couldn't talk or move on my own during that time, but I was very conscious of what was going on around me while in the intensive care unit

I heard nurses and doctors talking about me. I was aware that something traumatic had happened, but I still didn't know what it was. I later learned that doctors fought to restore stability to my blood pressure and rid me of an infection during my recuperation. In post-operative medical reports documenting my condition, physicians wrote, *"His hospital course was complicated by a labile* [fluctuating] *hypertension and decreased mental status, which steadily improved. He was extubated with difficulty on September 25.* [The doctors removed a tube they had inserted, but even that was complicated]. *The intracranial pressure bolt was removed and the patient was transferred to a room on the surgical floor on September 29.*

Sometime during that period a potentially life-threatening infection set in. By September 30, my temperature spiked to 101 degrees. Blood and urine cultures showed that the infection was caused by *Enterobacter aerogenes* bacteria. My doctors ordered antibiotic therapy. The combination of antibiotic medications they gave me gradually eliminated my fever. During the times that I was able to talk, I complained that my hands and lower arms hurt. That was the first pain I felt after the accident. I didn't know that it was "phantom pain" that amputees often feel.

In my dazed condition, I remembered winning first place in the biplane silver category at the Reno Air Races. What a thrill that was to finally reach top speed in my modified hand-built Pitts S1S. But how long ago was that? It seemed like yesterday. Mary Ann was with me in Reno, then we went home and she really didn't want me to go on this trip to Utah. She said she had bad feelings about it and pleaded with me to stay home. I was intent on going. We owned our house together and Mary Ann had picked up a will at a stationery store and urged me to sign it in case anything happened to me on this trip. I thought it was a little strange, because nothing was going to happen to me, but I signed it and headed for my Beechcraft Bonanza airplane at the Nut Tree Airport in Vacaville.

Sheila, who had stayed in Salt Lake City with Mary Ann for about four days, had to return to Vacaville to run her home furnishing import business, African Odyssey. When my blood pressure finally declined to a safe level and stabilized, and the swelling in my brain subsided, Mary Ann said she started rubbing my chest. The nurse stopped her, explaining that touching or rubbing is an irritant to the body of head injury patients. That really devastated her and at that point she said she felt completely helpless. All she could do was to sit there and look at me and try to talk to me, not knowing if I could hear or understand what she was saying.

We didn't have a cell phone in 1993, so all of the calls from concerned friends and family members were coming to Mary Ann through the hospital. The hospital staff seemed displeased by all of the calls, but those concerned calls were the only thing that kept Mary Ann grounded.

Mary Ann said that after a few days, I started holding up my bandaged arms and stared at them for hours at a time. About that time, my daughter, Shelley, flew up from Phoenix, and Mary Ann picked her up from the airport. They arrived in my room just after I had removed all of my bandages with my teeth. I don't remember a thing, but I guess my mangled arms looked raw and awful, and I was sorry that was the first thing my daughter saw. Nurses applied new bandages, but at every opportunity I unwrapped them again, then held up my arms in front of me and just stared at them. I was still numb physically and mentally, but even in my stupor I was trying to figure out what was going to happen after I left the hospital. How was I going to do anything without hands?

Following my move from intensive care into a regular hospital room, I had lots of daily appointments. The physical therapist told Mary Ann that a combination of head injury and loss of limbs normally throws off a person's balance, and that I would have to learn how to walk again. The therapist worked with us daily and showed Mary Ann how to hold a belt around my waist to steady me and help me walk.

Mary Ann said she gained a bit of hope when the psychologist tested me for cognitive flexibility. The psychologist asked, "Who is the president of the United States?" I answered, "Oh, he's married to Hillary." She said I was making jokes, but that I knew a lot of the things he was asking me. However, they told her if someone with a head injury had a short temper before the injury, it would be even worse after. That proved to be true in my case.

After two weeks, the medical staff told Mary Ann that they wanted me to remain in the Utah hospital for rehabilitation for the head injury. But, after living out of a suitcase, spending helpless days with me, and eating meals alone every night, Mary Ann was at her wit's end. She was mentally and physically exhausted, and went up to the nurse sobbing and pleading to let us go home.

The medical staff said I wasn't ready to go home, because every time Mary Ann took me out of my room in a wheelchair, I started screaming loudly that I was in pain. She said I never complained of pain when I was in bed, only when I was in the wheelchair. After one of my particularly loud, embarrassing episodes, Mary Ann said she got me back into bed, pulled me by the neck of my hospital gown and said, "If you don't knock this shit off, we are not going home. You are not in pain, and knock it off!" She asked me, "Do you want to go home?" I said, "Yes." She said, "Then shut up!" That wasn't like her at all. She was usually very positive and even-tempered, but she knew I wasn't actually in pain and that she had to treat me like a child to get my attention.

I spent three weeks in the hospital before I was finally discharged. Some friends Mary Ann had made in Salt Lake City agreed to take us to the airport. When I went out through the hospital doors, I emerged into what for me had become another world. Ten days earlier

13

I had been an airline pilot, and a competitive sport aviator—a guy who could do anything I felt like doing. During that ride from the hospital to the airport, I could only think of how helpless I suddenly was. That became increasingly apparent as soon as we arrived in the airport terminal building, when I announced, "I have to go to the bathroom." I was incapable of unzipping my pants, using the urinal, getting myself back in order or washing afterward. Our friend went into the men's bathroom to make sure no one was in there, and then stood guard at the door while Mary Ann helped me.

In the waiting area, I realized that people were staring at my bandaged stumps. I was no longer just a regular guy. I was handicapped, disabled. A double amputee. We finally got on the airplane bound for Sacramento. They put us in the first row, and almost immediately I started complaining, "I hurt!" Again, Mary Ann told me to "knock it off" or we weren't going home.

One of the flight attendants came over and—deliberately avoiding direct contact with me—asked Mary Ann, "Is he okay to fly?" Mary Ann said, "Yes. Please get me a glass of wine, and he'll have a Coke." Mary Ann held my Coke while I sipped it through a straw. I don't know how many blankets they put over me, but I felt so cold the whole flight from Salt Lake City to Sacramento.

The University of Utah had made arrangements for my immediate admission into the University of California, Davis, Medical Center in Sacramento, a major trauma treatment facility. Mary Ann said the University of Utah was wonderful, and everyone had been so caring and considerate. But she said the last thing she remembered was one of the nurses saying, "I hope you guys make it, because most couples don't in a situation like yours." Mary Ann knew she had a very long road ahead of her.

Throughout that flight home, I was haunted by a recurring dream that I had during my 10-day slumber in Utah. It was about my grandfather Samuel Penketh, who died in 1928 at 53 years of age, 18 years before I was born. When I was a child, my father had told me stories about how his father had been an engineer, and how he had lost use of his hand after getting it caught in some machinery while working for the railroad in Chicago. He never let that get in the way of his pursuits. He couldn't afford to, and besides that, he was too damned stubborn to let that little inconvenience get in his way.

I also remember dreaming about my father, who had died in 1968, when I was 21. He was way too young to die at 58 years old, and so was I at 47. But I couldn't imagine how I was going to survive. I found the enormity of my plight so paralyzing, the prospect of my future so incomprehensible, that I turned to thoughts of my past with my father for solace.

Chapter 2

A Rich Man's Sport

My father, George Penketh, grew up in Michigan, and my mother, Leonne Theresa Baltes, was originally from Madison, Wisconsin. During World War II, my dad was a Marine and served as an aviation machinist mate, commonly known as an airplane mechanic. He was stationed at the Goleta Marine Corps Air Station in Santa Barbara, California. My mom gave birth to my brother there in 1945, but he died shortly after he was born.

After World War II, my parents moved to Chicago so my dad could reclaim his old job as a postman. I was born on July 23, 1946, in Oak Park, Illinois—a suburb of Chicago—but I claim California as my home state, since I lived in Illinois for only a few months. Chicago winters were harsh, and my parents had been spoiled by sunny California so, soon after I was born, they moved to the Los Angeles area—first to the community of Gardena and later to Whittier, where I grew up. My father had two jobs—he was a postman and he worked afternoons as a truck driver making parcel pick-ups and deliveries.

I was almost four years old on June 25, 1950, the day that marked the beginning of the Korean War. My father, who had been recalled for Marine service duty, joined the U.S. Marine Corps Squadron VMF-214— the Black Sheep Squadron. He told me so many stories about Corsairs and the Black Sheep Squadron, and its famous leader, Pappy Boyington. My father was on the USS Sicily aircraft carrier—CVE 118, a very small carrier. They called ships of its size "baby flat tops." The skipper of the USS Sicily was Jimmy Thatch, who had been a Naval aviator during World War II. He became famous for developing the "Thatch Weave," a defensive formation used in air combat. The Thatch Weave improved the ability of U.S. Navy planes to combat the highly maneuverable Japanese Zeros, which saved many American lives.

Although I had heard lots of stories about airplanes,

I still hadn't been around them until my dad returned from Korea. He was on active duty in 1951 when he took me out to El Toro Marine Corps Air Station and showed me an F4UB Corsair. It was the biggest thing I'd ever seen. Although it wasn't that big by today's standards, it appeared enormous to me. I remember he picked me up and put me in the cockpit, and I cried because I was so scared. I was so high up—probably 10 feet off the ground. I yelled and cried until he took me out of the cockpit. But over the following months interest replaced fear as my dad took me to see many other aircraft.

By kindergarten, I had more knowledge about airplanes than anybody in my school. I remember going to kindergarten

My parents, George Penketh and Leonne Theresa Baltes

19

and telling all the kids what an R2800 was. I told them that Korean Corsairs have four 20 millimeter cannons rather than six 50-caliber machine guns, and that Corsairs were the first aircraft to go over 400 miles an hour. I knew who Jimmy Thatch was, I knew who Pappy Boyington was. I got in trouble in kindergarten telling the kids what a "bastard stripe" was. It's the black stripe—the Black Sheep insignia. When the Black Sheep Squadron was founded in 1943, Pappy Boyington was such a charismatic leader, the guys wanted to name the squadron "Boyington's Bastards." Of course, that would never be approved, so they named it the Black Sheep Squadron. The Black Sheep Squadron had such great stories to tell that Hollywood made a television series that started in September 1976 starring Robert Conrad as Major Greg "Pappy" Boyington.

Building model airplanes was a natural progression for me. Initially, with three two-by-fours and a few nails, I had an airplane. Those masterpieces soon gave way to gas-powered control-line flying models. I still remember being about 9 years old, riding my bike several miles to Jack's Hobby Shop in Whittier. I would spent the better part of an hour carefully inspecting the available kits for sale. Probably a good part of that time I was in deep thought or dreaming of winging my way through the sky. It was a big choice—a Ringmaster Junior or a Flight Streak Junior. Proudly, I would walk up to Jack or his wife, Doris, at the counter and present my choice. Jack would say, "That'll be $2.01 ($1.95 for the kit and 6 cents tax, 3 percent in those days). Do you need any glue?" I would then venture back into the aisles and pick up a tube of Ambroid glue, a Veco bell crank and control horn, and some piano wire for push rods and lead-outs.

With a new kit tucked under my arm, the bike ride home always seemed fast. After parking my bike, it was off to the airplane factory—better known as my bedroom. During the summer months, with no school, airplanes became my life. My desk was covered with tools of my trade—newspapers, pins, a soft board where I pinned freshly glued parts, sandpaper, super-sharp X-acto knives and, of course, a supply of Band-Aids. Everything in my room became coated in balsa wood dust. Even though my mother was a very clean housekeeper, she accommodated me by looking the other way. After my dad arrived home from work, he would always pass through the "airplane factory," checking on my progress. I was so fortunate to have two of the greatest parents who ever lived!

Next to my dust-covered bed was a stack of MAN (*Model Airplane News*) magazines. The dog-eared pages always led to the engine advertisements. I did not yet have the proper engine for these magnificent airplanes. My dad would often sit and look at these magazines with me, and quiz me on things like, "How big is that engine? How many rpm's? What's its weight? What size prop do you need?"

One day, my dad walked into my room and handed me a paper bag, saying, "This is an early birthday present." (Six months early! What a dad!) The bag contained a familiar-looking black and green box. It was a K&B Torpedo .19 gas airplane engine! Suddenly I had the power to zoom away.

As a kid, I was obsessed not only by airplanes but also by baseball. I think my interest in baseball was inspired by watching the television series **Leave it to Beaver**, which ran from 1957 to 1963. I remember an episode showing Beaver running home and saying, "Mom, I made the team!" I wanted to go home and say, "Hey, mom, I made the team!" When I went out for Little League tryouts, I wanted to be a pitcher. But they didn't have a third baseman, so I said, "I'm a third baseman!" But I'd never played. So I went out in the field and stood on third base—which, of course, isn't the way to play third base. So then the coach said, "You ever play third base?" I said, "No." But that didn't stop me. How do you learn anything without just going for it? That would prove to be my motto for the rest of my life.

I really wanted to be a pitcher after playing third base, so my dad took me aside and said, "If you want to be a pitcher, we'll make you a pitcher." That winter, my dad and I started practicing out in the driveway, and I pitched 100 balls every night. During the next five years, I became a very good pitcher. My dad didn't know how to play baseball—he was learning, too. I remember he painted home plate and the pitcher's rubber on the driveway, with the proper 46-foot pitching distance for Little League minors, 54 feet for juniors, and 60 feet 6 inches for major league. He bought me all kinds of books, and I studied them. I pitched a fastball. I practiced the Stan Williams no-windup pitch for a while. Stan Williams was a Dodgers pitcher—number 40. I went down to Wrigley Field in 1958, the year the Dodgers came out to Los Angeles. I was 12 years old. They had a winter league team that played there called the Dodger

Juniors. They had Sandy Koufax, Don Drysdale, Ed Roebuck, Ron Fairly, Jim Gilliam, Frank Howard, Johnny Roseboro, Gil Hodges, Don Zimmer, Carl Furillo, Duke Snider, Pee Wee Reese, Johnny Podres, Carl Erskine, Don Newcombe and Ed Palmquist. I was their bat boy, their clubhouse boy, and their gopher. I was thrilled when they let me pitch batting practice with them.

My dad and I went to Dodgers baseball games every week. I remember my mom and dad would call each other during the daytime to go to the game, and my mom and I would take the bus down to Los Angeles, and meet my dad at the Los Angeles Coliseum.

I played baseball all the way through high school—three years of varsity—and into my first year of college. I was the same size then as I am now, 5 feet 9 inches, and I watched as everyone else grew bigger than me. In high school that's not a bad size, but when you get in college, you're now a little guy. I played semi-pro baseball every winter. I played for the Detroit Tigers Juniors league and I played with the semi-pros for awhile, but I knew that my pitching days were numbered.

The last game I pitched was in Montebello, when I was with the Pacific Clay Yankees. We played a team in Montebello that was really good, with some minor leaguers on it. I pitched 10 innings with 12 strikeouts, but we lost the game in the 10th inning on a home run. There were always baseball scouts in the stands. In those days, the scouts would wear those felt hats with the brim, and they would stand out like a sore thumb. We used to go to Anaheim to the American Legion Tournament every year. We'd always see the scouts there, and I'd ask them for their business cards. At that last game, several scouts were in the stands, and I pitched my best game ever. But nobody said a word to me. So I said, "That's all I got. It's the best I can do," and that was the last game I played. It was a big disappointment for me, but airplanes remained a big interest in my life. And I was becoming fascinated by cars.

I entered my senior year of high school in the fall of 1963. I'll never forget that November 22, sitting in a class called Senior Problems taught by Mr. Chandler, when just before noon he answered the classroom telephone. He then walked outside the classroom and returned with a look of shock and anguish. He said to us, "The flag is at half mast. Our president has been assassinated in Dallas, Texas."

My parents always had impressed upon me the necessity of an education. I, too, realized the importance of completing high school and college. I had only one problem—I didn't know what I wanted to be when I grew up.

Sitting one afternoon in the library looking through college catalogs, it was as if I was hit by lightning when I noticed that Mount San Antonio College in Walnut, California, offered a commercial aviation program, designed to lead to a career as a professional airline pilot. Why hadn't I thought of this? As much as I was interested in shop classes, baseball, girls and cars in high school, my passion for flying burned with a brighter flame. I thought to myself, "This is a golden opportunity—going to college to study airplanes!" It was a great way to go to school. I figured I might as well take courses in something I liked—it made school easier.

That evening, at the dinner table, I proudly informed my parents that I would soon be off for college and I would be an airline pilot. My dad gave me that look that only dads can give saying, "You'd *better* go to college." My decision to pursue pilot training through an accredited college program obviously impressed him.

My father always told me flying airplanes was a rich man's sport. The first time I ever flew was during my first flying lesson in 1964 at Fallin Air Services located on Commonwealth Avenue on the south side of Fullerton Airport. My first flight instructor was a guy named Bill Vanderlinden. Bill answered all my questions, told me about the Cessna 150 and the requirements for a private pilot's license. He then asked me a simple question: "Why do you want to take flying lessons?" I replied, "So I can be an airline pilot." Bill smiled and asked if I had ever been in an airplane. I replied, "No. Is that a requirement to take lessons?" A couple of days later my first time in an airplane also became my first flying lesson.

Just as that first gas model airplane engine gave me the power to zoom away, my first flying lesson gave me a chance to soar with eagles.

After high school I had a job at a drive-in dairy, but my father said, "As long as you stay in college, I will help pay for your flying lessons." He gave me $100 per month, and in those days, that was a lot of money to fly airplanes.

In the mid-1960s flying was relatively inexpensive, compared to today. I remember a Cessna 150 training aircraft rented for $12 an hour for solo and $14 an hour for dual instruction. They offered a 10 percent discount for buying a $100 block of flying time.

I trained on Cessna 150s—100-horsepower, little bitty airplanes—but at Fullerton Airport I saw an assortment of airplanes that stirred my imagination. I flew every one of them—in my mind. I was a dreamer. I remember a yellow J3 Cub sitting on the green grass, a Porterfield, an SNJ Trainer, a Fletcher COIN Fighter, and off in the corner a Curtiss P-40 Tomahawk. I sat many hours in the P-40 imagining—I was a Flying Tiger in China. I was Pappy Boyington's wingman. I was an ace!

Meanwhile that summer, halfway around the world, real fighter pilots found themselves engaged in a conflict that soon would affect the lives of millions of people and alter the American political landscape for the next decade.

An incident between the North Vietnamese and the U.S. destroyers Maddox and Turner Joy in the Gulf of Tonkin escalated the Vietnam conflict. Lieutenant Commander Everett Alvarez, Jr., was shot down and captured August 5, 1964, on the first raid in North Vietnam in retaliation for the attack. Alvarez was the longest-held POW in North Vietnam—he was a prisoner for eight and a half years.

When I entered college in September 1964, I was given class credit for my flying lessons. Imagine, a college elective credit for flying airplanes! I earned one unit for each 15 hours I flew with a maximum of three units per semester, and my flight instructor assigned the grade. What a boost for the ol' GPA!

School studies went along okay, but flying lessons were exceptional. My GPA benefited, and by the end of the first semester, I had a private pilot's ticket in my back pocket. About this time I began to seriously look at a career as an airline pilot. In those days the published minimum requirements to be hired appeared deceivingly simple: 18 years old, passage of a first-class medical examination, a commercial license and an instrument rating. I still had three semesters ahead of me—more than enough time to meet these minimum requirements. I would have to fight 'em off with a stick. Ah...such a naive young man.

After I got my associate's degree and had obtained the basic requirements to be hired by the airlines, I sent applications to almost every airline in the world—with no response. Soon I realized that there was a huge difference between minimum and competitive requirements to be hired by a major airline. In the meantime, I had earned my flight instructor's rating and set off to log additional flying hours in quest of that elusive airline job. I also started classes at California State University, Fullerton, but trying to hold down a full-time job as a flight instructor at Fullerton Airport and attend classes at the same time became very difficult. Furthermore, my attention was distracted by another lingering interest.

I always liked hot rods. In high school I drove a 1930 Model A Ford deluxe coupe with a rumble seat that often had a surfboard sticking out of it. I later replaced the Model A with a 1955 Ford Thunderbird convertible. While I was taking flying lessons at Fullerton Airport, I met a guy named Jack Lufkin, who was manager for Ak Miller Garage, a business that built and worked on race cars. The name of the garage came from its owner, famous race car driver Ak Miller. Both Miller and Lufkin were involved in land speed racing at Bonneville in Utah, where over the years the Miller/Lufkin/Carr team set and reset numerous records.

I went to Bonneville for the first time with Jack when I was a senior in high school. I was his "gopher"— an errand boy hired to "go for" items or chores. I wiped the salt off the tires, and was told to get this, get that. We stayed overnights in Wendover, Nevada. I went to Bonneville for two or three years as a young man, then I stopped going. Still, the hook was set in 1964, and in the back of my mind I always recalled how much I really enjoyed it. The lure would call me back to Bonneville in 1991.

Chapter 3

Nuclear Weapons and Napalm

Other things began to alter my airline career plans. By 1966, the little skirmish in Southeast Asia was heating up, my II-S student deferment was getting weak, and the Selective Service Board had begun the draft lottery program, using birth dates to determine pools of people to be called up for military duty. By the time I earned my associate in arts degree in 1966, I had almost 2,000 hours of flight time, but the airlines still wouldn't talk to me. I didn't fancy being drafted because I didn't find the idea of carrying an M14 rifle through rice paddies attractive. I devised what I thought would be an effective way to avoid the Vietnam War. I simply joined the Marine Corps Reserve. In those days it was extremely rare for any reserve unit to be activated. I figured on boot camp, six months of active duty, then one weekend of service a month until my six-year obligation was over. Then I would finish school, get married, raise a family and have a normal life. But I've never been accused of being normal.

I went to Los Alamitos Naval Air Station and this gunnery sergeant pumped me full of BS. He said, "You're going to have a great time...." So I took my dad down there and my dad asked, "Can I re-enlist?" He was too old; but I enlisted. I'll never forget that morning in September 1966 when I reported for duty at Los Alamitos, where the other recruits and I were instructed to board a bus bound for the Marine Corps Recruiting Depot in San Diego. I was one of the older guys in the group, so the gunnery sergeant gave me the paperwork for everyone in the group. He also gave me a dime and said, "When you get down to the bus station in San Diego, put this dime in the phone and call this number and tell them that you're there." So we got off the bus and I said, "Hang on, you guys, I'm supposed to call the base and check in to tell them that we're here." So I put the dime in and called that number, and some guy answered and yelled at me so loud I had to move the phone about two feet from

Platoon 2245 at Camp Pendleton in 1966

my ear. He called me every name in the book. I thought to myself, "This is a mistake!" He finally said, "I want every f-ing one of you assholes at the curb at attention right now!" I walked out and said to the guys, "I think we made a big mistake. They told us to be on the curb and at attention and they'll send a bus to pick us up." The bus pulled up—a small, gray Navy bus. Out comes a big black guy about eight feet tall. He just looks at us and says, "Is that attention? I wouldn't want to be the last swinging dick to get on this bus." We got in that bus so fast! He looked at us and all he said was, "Shut up!" We all sat there, and I was thinking, "Man, I really screwed up this time." So we drove into the gate at the Marine Corps

Recruit Depot and they took us to the receiving barracks. The bus stopped at these yellow painted footprints. The door opened and the drill sergeant says, "I wouldn't want to be the last maggot to stand on those footprints." So we stood on those footprints at attention in the hot sun for about three hours.

That was only the start. They shave your head and then you take all of your clothes off and take a shower. You put everything you have with you in a box and mail it home. Then you go and you're issued a utility uniform. Everything you need is provided for you. You have no identity. At that point you're lower than whale dung, the lowest thing on Earth because it sinks to the bottom of the ocean. When you join the Air Force you're an airman, when you join the Navy you're a sailor, when you join the Army you're a soldier, but when you join the Marine Corps, you're lower than whale dung. You get the title of "Marine" only after you graduate from boot camp. Only after you earn the title of Marine are you allowed to call yourself a Marine.

I was in Platoon 2245 at Marine Corps Recruit Depot. In boot camp, you learn how important your fellow Marine is—it's all teamwork for 10 weeks, 18 hours a day. You barely have time to get your butts in

Aviation Machinst's Mate A School in 1967

the chairs for your first meal and the drill instructor says, "You'd better suck it up now, because you're done, you're out of here."

They say the only way out of Marine boot camp is to graduate or die. And they're pretty much right. In those days the drill instructors could swear, which they're not supposed to do these days. As recruits, we were not allowed to speak to our drill instructor without asking for permission. Only after graduation could we address him as "sergeant," and only then would he finally speak to us without swearing at us. My father was at my graduation from boot camp, and he knew what I went through.

As a reservist, after finishing boot camp, I was able

37

to choose the aviation maintenance field. The remaining 80 percent of my training platoon members were off to infantry training regiment (ITR) at Camp Pendelton—then an almost sure trip to Vietnam. I often wonder whatever happened to those fellow Marines. One in particular was Private General Pierce. Yes, that was his full name—"General Pierce." General Pierce was a good man, a black Marine from the South. With a name like that, he had a rough time getting through boot camp. I didn't help him out. I treated him badly from the day I met him. I was an ignorant young man. If I had a choice to meet only one member of that group of 80 Marines today, it would be Private General Pierce. I owe him an apology.

My training took me to Jacksonville, Florida, for basic mechanic school, then to Memphis, Tennessee, for aviation jet mechanic school. Soon I returned to Los Alamitos Naval Air Station, where I became an A-4 plane captain with the Marine Attack Squadron VMA-241. I was a year or so older than my enlisted contemporaries, but still a few years younger than our junior pilots.

Most of our pilots had flown in Vietnam and had embarked on their airline pilot careers. It was a sunny Sunday afternoon as I sat on an A-4 boarding ladder talking to one of our pilots. We talked of airline jobs, flying experience, our futures and such. I almost fell off the ladder when he told me he had flown the F-8 Crusader, supersonic, off carriers, yet he had only about 1,500 hours of flight time. I was still instructing at Fallin Air Service and had about 3,000 hours of flight time. A change was in the making.

I met my first wife, Hillary Christian, in high school. Back then, we were only acquaintances. Both of us had

Mike and Hillary, Christmas 1968

attended California High School in Whittier and graduated in 1964. I didn't see Hillary again until I got back from boot camp and was attending Rio Hondo College taking night classes. I ran into her while switching classes. We started dating in 1968 and got married shortly after. I was working as a flight instructor at Fallin Air Service for $5 per hour, still trying to get an airline job.

One winter day at Fullerton Airport early in 1970 while we were socked in with fog and I was waiting to go flying and make some money, I called up the Marine Corps recruiter. I asked, "Are you guys hiring pilots?" He said, "Yes, sir. Tell me more." I said, "I'm a PFC in the Marine Corps out of Los Alamitos, and I'm an A-4 plane captain. I'm a pilot and a flight instructor, and I'd like to go fly in the Marine Corps." He said, "We sure are hiring pilots. Do you have two years of college?" I said, "Yes, I do." He said, "Come on down!" So I went down to see him the next morning. He offered me a sales pitch I couldn't refuse. He said, "We've got a program called the Aviation Scholarship Program, which is for two-year college grads." So I took a battery of tests and he said, "These are the highest scores we've ever seen!" I said, "Great!" Looking back on it now, I think he probably told this to everyone.

I always was thrilled—and somewhat amused— that people would pay me to fly airplanes. I would gladly have paid them. Imagine—a 24-year-old kid, a super-sonic jet, and a government credit card!

OCS, Quantico, Virginia, 1970

The next question was, "When?" I was ready on the spot, but the next opening for OCS (Officer Candidates School in Quantico, Virginia) would be in about six weeks. I had forgotten one thing, a very important thing. I had not told my wife, Hillary, of my new venture. "Mmm," I thought, "I'd better tell her."

Hillary was working as a drive-up teller at a Bank of America branch in La Habra, California. On the way home from the recruiting station, I drove up to her window and announced, "I've just joined the Marines!" She replied, "You're already a Marine!" I said, "No. It's a little different this time; I leave in six weeks for OCS in Quantico, Virginia."

We were living in a condominium in Fullerton at the time. There wasn't a whole lot she could say about it, but she seemed to understand. She had been a "Navy brat." Her father, Custer Christian, was a retired gunner's mate, a battleship sailor, in World War II. I regret never having spent any time with her father. He had died shortly after we married, and I never got to really know him. Only now do I realize what he did and the history that surrounded him. Like my father, who died about the same time, these proud men lived through incredible times—the Prohibition days, the stock market crash, World War II, Korea—their stories are gone forever.

Six weeks after enrolling in the Aviation Scholarship Program, in the spring of 1970, I drove my 1965 Corvette on Route 66 back to Quantico, Virginia, to Officer Candidates School. There I had the rudest awakening of my life.

Officer Candidates School was one of the most difficult challenges I'd ever faced. The boot camp that I went through for recruit training in 1966 was a group project. The group went through together, and the group graduated together. However, at OCS, it was all individual, and it was extremely difficult. With a group, you get peer support. In OCS, you get peer ratings. Your peers grade you. You're graded on leadership qualities and all kinds of stuff. If you flunked out of OCS, you went back to the enlisted Marine Corps, and that didn't appeal to me at all.

Mike in Pensacola

At boot camp, you take direction from "drill instructors," and you call them "sir." At OCS they're called "sergeant instructors," and you never call them "sir." I remember the first week I was there, they told us we were going on a conditioning hike, and although I had tried to get in good physical shape before I got there, I had no idea what was in store for me. I found out when the sergeant instructor said, "We're going to go on a conditioning hike on the hill trail. It's about six miles." It was six miles—straight up and straight down in mud at a trot. Conditioning, my ass! It about killed me! But somehow I got through that and other rigorous OCS drills, and was commissioned second lieutenant in November 1970.

Hillary came back to Quantico for my graduation and then we moved down to Pensacola, Florida—the first in a series of moves for flight school training. New second lieutenants had about two weeks' delay before reporting to flight school in Pensacola. Most guys went home in their uniform with a couple of butter bars on their shoulder, told their parents how cool they were, and talked to their high school and college buddies. I got commissioned on a Friday, but on Monday morning I checked into the Marine Aviation Department (MAD) in Pensacola, because I wanted to fly airplanes. The major at MAD looked at my orders and said, "You're not supposed to be here for two weeks." I said, "Yes, sir, but I wanted to come down here and fly airplanes. I didn't come down here to go on leave." So they sent me to Saufley Field, where I joined my first Navy Training Squadron VT-1. I was to start ground school and fly the T-34 Beechcraft Mentor. By the time the other guys from my OCS school got there, I was halfway through the initial phase of training. It was absolutely great!

I'd say 95 percent of student aviators had never been in an airplane in their life. I'd already had over 3,000 hours and an Air Transport Pilot rating. The Beechcraft

Navy 2-seater VT-1

T-34 is propeller-driven airplane with tandem seating, and a 225-horse Continental engine. I remember the first flight. I was with my flight instructor, Navy Lieutenant Finnicaro, and we started the airplane and he showed me how to taxi. I said, "Great. Can I try it?" He said, "No. I don't let my students taxi on the first flight." So we took off and he climbed the airplane to about 3,000 feet, showing me what the ailerons, elevator, rudder and controls do. After he showed me how to work the controls he asked, "You want to fly it now?" I said, "Yes, sir." He said, "Okay. Are you ready?" I said, "Yes, sir."

He said, "Okay. You got it!" I said, "Yes, sir, I've got it!" He asked, "You got it?" I said, "Yes sir, why?" He said, "Nothing's happening." I said, "Is something supposed to happen? You told me to keep the wings level and go straight ahead. That's what we're doing." He said, "Try a turn." So I tried a couple of turns and he asked, "Have you flown before?" I said, "Yes, sir. I've flown a little bit." So then he started showing me some aerobatics, and he got rather aggressive showing me more challenging aerobatic maneuvers with the airplane—rolls and loops. He showed me a point roll. That's a maneuver in which you rotate the plane 90 degrees and stop when the airplane is in knife-edge position, then 90 degrees to inverted, another 90 degrees to knife-edge, and right side up. He asked, "How did you like that?" I said, "Pretty good, but you need a little bit of top rudder though knife edge." He said, "What?" I said, "Well, the nose fell out. A little top rudder will keep the nose on the horizon." We had a great time after that. He was a good guy and we worked well together.

Reassignment to different bases was called PCS (permanent change of station) orders, and for me there would be many of them. After VT-1 at Pensacola, and Saufley Field where I got to fly the Beechcraft T-34 Mentor for about eight weeks, my next PCS orders took me to Meridian, Mississippi, for training in Squadron VT-7. Although we always referred to the base as Meridian, its formal name was McCain Naval Air Station (named after John McCain's father). That training included basic jet transition, formation flying and instruments. I flew the single-engine T2A Buckeye for about 15 weeks. Also in Meridian, I went down the hall in the same hangar to the VT-9 Squadron for advanced formation and instrument flying. I flew the twin-engine T2B-T2C Buckeye for about 15 weeks. Hillary and I had an apartment in Meridian, and while we were there our daughter, Shelley Diane, was born on May 5, 1971. Hillary and I stayed together only until about 1974. The split and eventual divorce was due to my own immaturity.

From Meridian, I traveled back to Pensacola Naval Air Station (Forrest Sherman Field) to join VT-4 training squadron for my initial aircraft carrier qualification and air-to-air gunnery training. There I flew the twin-engine T2C Buckeye for about four weeks. Finally, I engaged in advanced flight training with VT-22 squadron in Kingsville, Texas, where I flew Douglas TA4F and J Skyhawks for another 15 weeks. It was absolutely incredible! It's the biggest thrill I've ever had. We did carrier landing practices called FCLPs (field carrier landing practice) at several OLFs (outlying landing fields). We'd go out for about a dozen 45-minute sessions and all we did was practice landings. We had a landing signal officer (LSO) who watched every landing. He had what we called a Mark-20 eyeball. He knew exactly what we were doing, and he knew how fast we were going—to the knot. He could tell if we were two knots fast.

You don't know what it's like to land on an aircraft carrier until you do it. When I checked in at Pensacola, I noticed the USS Lexington, a training carrier, tied up to the dock in Pensacola Bay. I knew that I would be landing on her decks on some distant day in the future, but my wait turned out to be less than five months.

I still remember that day, saluting the gate guards and driving through the gates of Sherman Field—the next stop being VT-4 operations. The VT-4 was the training squadron for initial carrier qualification. As I entered the VT-4 "ready room," the students there seemed to be in either of two different groups—those who had qualified, and those waiting to go aboard the boat.

A squadron briefing, a discussion on course rules, was followed by ground school on the T2C, which had a slightly newer airframe than that of the T2B. It also had a different engine, a gun sight and a 50 mm gun pod under each wing. The next day, we were scheduled for our first dual familiarization flight with an instructor. However, most FCLPs and *all* actual carrier landings are done solo when you're a student. There is no instructor dumb enough to fly with a student aboard the boat!

The weather in the Florida panhandle was beautiful. I remember lush green fields, white puffy clouds, crystal white sandy beaches and the deep blue ocean. But what really got my attention was watching the Lexington head out of Pensacola Bay toward the big, blue ocean. There is only one reason the Lexington leaves port: to participate in training drills. I was scheduled for a solo flight the next day.

Every Navy carrier landing is the same. It's like a crash landing—you come in on a three-point landing (all three wheels touch the deck at the same time) and basically crash the airplane on the runway. It's all in preparation for landing on the boat. You try to develop a habit before going to the boat. The boat is moving, it may have a pitching deck with rough seas, and you have to make that landing. You can't make a mistake!

I was 24 years old at the time, and bullet-proof! Nothing was going to happen to me. If I thought something was going to happen to me, I wouldn't have been there. I heard stories of student Naval aviators who failed—one student taxied off the carrier deck and they never found him. The deck of the carrier is probably 100 feet above the water and the boat is moving. They recovered the airplane, but he ejected underwater but the canopy and seat and were never found.

After becoming field-qualified, I now awaited the actual carrier qualification. I was nervous as we waited—just like everyone else. The night before my flight, I had dinner at the club, as did most of the other guys, and planned an early evening in preparation for an 0700 briefing. A good night's sleep was wishful thinking. I was up every hour, checking the time, walking over to the window for a weather check. Finally I gave up, got up, put on my uniform and walked to the weather office at station operations.

It's not common to find a junior officer checking the weather at 0200. I walked into the weather office, where a senior chief was on duty, and said, "Good morning, chief." He replied, "Good morning, sir" (he must have been twice my age). Trying to look mature and nonchalant, I asked about the weather forecast for the approaching daylight hours. I thought, mmm, good weather as far as I can see. We exchanged a little more small talk, and I thanked him for the report and turned to leave. As I opened the door, the chief smiled and said, "Oh, Lieutenant, 50 miles off the beach you'll find calm seas. Expect a steady deck." These ol' salts, they know what's going on.

The brief was at 0700, a flight of four, and I was to be the LSO's wingman. We were briefed on the departure, rendezvous, en route procedures and formations, and a textbook 250-knot, 5-second interval break. We were told to expect a "Charlie" time of about 0930. The LSO would trap (an arrested landing) on his first pass under the guidance of the ship's LSO. Meanwhile, we would make two touch-and-goes (with the ship's LSO) while our LSO manned his position.

The weather en route was beautiful at FL180, with clear blue skies, unlimited visibility, a layer of puffy white clouds at about 10,000 feet. After departure our leader crossed the second section over by giving us a hand signal (a raised fist moved vertically) and moving us into a loose cruise formation. It was common to conduct an entire flight in radio silence using hand signals that were common to all Marine and Navy pilots. For the first time in many hours, I finally took a deep breath!

Traveling at 4 to 5 nautical miles per minute (240–300 knots per hour), we covered the approximately 50-mile distance to the boat fast. As our lead contacted the ship, he moved us to a right echelon formation. Our lead received a revised Charlie time of 0938, and got a heading and distance to the ship. Moments later, the lead called his flight and said the ship was 10 o'clock about 20 miles. As we pushed over, I kept searching the seemingly empty horizon, and then I finally spotted something. I was shocked. A fly speck was bigger than that boat! And they expect *me* to land on *that*!

Wes Pac, Iwakuni, Japan, A-4E with 20 mm cannon

Life is nothing but a series of challenges, one after the other. This was just another challenge for me. Imagine the typical student naval aviator: 22–24 years old, college graduate, typically a hard-charger type of personality. His entire flight experience totals about 175 hours and here he sits solo, in a twin-engine jet, descending at 300 knots toward a fly speck in the ocean. In an hour or so he will be the proudest man alive. He will have done something accomplished by about only 1 percent of all aviators in the world. He will be a qualified carrier pilot.

Prior to landing on the boat, four wires are stretched across the width of the carrier. To make the perfect landing, the goal is to trap the third wire. Every pass is televised throughout the entire ship, and you're graded on every pass. To qualify for a carrier landing, we needed six successful traps. I did six traps in a T-2C and, in advanced training, six traps in a TA-4 Skyhawk. A lot of people don't realize that when you're out there on final approach—say you're a quarter of a mile out— the window you have to go through narrows as you approach the ship. When you're just off the deck, that window tapers to about five square feet. So that's the funnel you have to go through. That's how precise you have to be. The initial carrier qualification is always done in VFR (visual flight rules) conditions.

Each trap is followed by a catapult shot ("cat" shot), which is the way you take off from a carrier. It is an incredible feeling. After my first carrier landing, I was taxiing toward the port cat thinking, "I wish I had time to pinch myself to see if I'm still alive. Time? Naw—there just isn't time as I'm positioned on the catapult. The take-off ramp on the Lexington carrier is probably about 200 feet long, and you accelerate from 0 to 140 knots within that distance. You're absolutely helpless. The shooter—the catapult officer—then owns you. You have control over the power, but a deck crewman using a tiller bar steers your nose wheel onto the catapult shuttle. You have a holdback fitting in the back of the airplane, which is a cast piece of metal with a certain shear strength. It's affixed to the airplane and anchored by a cable to the deck. When the catapult thrust exceeds the shear strength of the holdback bar, the metal bar breaks and you're slammed forward into the sky. As you ready for the cat shot, you put your right elbow into your side because if you don't have your elbow in, it may jerk back during the cat shot. If your elbow is out while you're gripping the stick, you might pull back on it because of the instant acceleration, causing you to over-rotate the aircraft at minimum speed. So you hold your elbow in and just cup your right hand behind the stick, and as the aircraft accelerates the stick is thrust into your cupped hand. Now for the left hand. The pilot grabs both the throttle and a cat grip—which is a fixed handle attached to the side of the cockpit—to prevent his hand from pulling back on the throttle and reducing power when maximum thrust is required. A carrier deck is the most dangerous flying spot in the world.

When you launch, you have to have your head against the headrest or your head will slam back so hard it will crack your helmet. When you're positioned in the catapult, the ground crew runs around the aircraft checking for leaks or anything obviously wrong. If everything checks out, they give you a thumbs-up. You sit there and put your elbow in your sides, your head against the head rest and look at the catapult officer out there and give him a quick salute—that means you're ready. And you just wait with your engine revved up to full power. Your ass belongs to him at that point, and you can't do anything except go for a ride. The acceleration is like nothing you have ever felt. In less than a split second, you are clear of the deck, the stick falls back into your hand, and you're flying.

Time to do it again, and again—until six traps are completed. The drinks are on you at the club tonight!

After I got my wings, I could have picked anywhere I wanted to be stationed, so I picked El Toro because I wanted to go back to Southern California. I checked into El Toro, and they asked, "What airplane do you want?" I said, "I want F-4 Phantoms." They said, "We have a three-month wait to get into VMAT 101 training for F-4 Phantoms. You can have VMAT 102 with A-4s right now, though." When I looked at the board and saw that one of the A-4 squadrons was my dad's old squadron—VMF 214—I said, "I'll take the A-4s now." I was sent to the Marine Corps Air Station in Yuma, Arizona, where I joined the VMAT Marine Attack Training Squadron 102. The "F" in VMF stood for "fighter," and 214 was later changed to VMA, which is designated "attack."

When you get out of flight school, you have just the bare minimum in knowledge and skills required for flying military aircraft. It's not until you are assigned to a squadron that you really get involved with the airplane. You do a lot of air-to-ground delivery of rockets, bombs, air-to-air guns, instrument flying, formation flying—you really fine-tune all of those skills. We flew the single-seat A-4 Echo, and I was there for about six months. Then I returned to El Toro and joined squadron 214 Black Sheep, and the training continued flying the A4F and A4M. To qualify to go to West Pac (West Pacific) we had to qualify in MOS (Military Occupational Specialty)

7592, a designation for special weapons delivery. I was training to deliver nuclear weapons and spent the next six months doing that—all we did was train. We practiced dropping ordnance on targets in the desert around Yuma and in Nevada. We dropped a lot of live ordnance around the Chocolate Mountains, by the Salton Sea. We did a lot of low-level navigation practice all over the country (often in desert areas) using only a compass and stopwatch at 500 feet (we sometimes flew lower) to simulate radar avoidance. We didn't have any of the modern navigation equipment they have today. It was all manual. We would take a map and draw a line on it and make two-minute tick marks. We went 360 knots or 10 seconds per mile—that's six miles a minute. So every two minutes we had a checkpoint, and our goal was to hit those checkpoints to the second on course. If you were 10 seconds fast, you'd learn how to adjust, and pick it up the next time. The time had to be precise because if you were going to drop a nuclear weapon, you had to have that bomb impact timed to the second. On a special weapons delivery, we had to accelerate from 360 to 500 knots to deliver a weapon. You knew the distance, time and fuel burn for that acceleration. And if you accelerate to that speed, you went from an initial point—IP—to the target. At the IP point we clicked on the LABS weapon delivery system and that would time the drop.

My West Pac orders assigned me to Iwakuni, Japan, near Hiroshima. After being based in Iwakuni, I went on to Okinawa, Taiwan and the Philippines. Initially I was to join the Tomcats VMA-311 attack squadron for a year in Okinawa. But after six months of flying, they sent me to Camp Hansen and made me a forward air controller (FAC). I wasn't too happy because a pilot doesn't want to be on the ground. They would give me a couple of days every month to fly with 311, and I'll never forget one flight.

I took off from Naha Air Base in Okinawa with a full load of live ordnance, including napalm, bombs, and 20 millimeter cannon shells on a mission to practice bombing some little island out in the Pacific. The A4 had one generator for power—no battery. If you lost the generator, you had a ram air turbine (RAT) you would deploy. It was a wind-driven generator that popped out with propeller blades on it. The air would spin the propeller on the RAT, supplying minimal electrical power to fly the airplane. The engine was started in the first place with an external starter and an electrical power supply, so you couldn't self-start the airplane. On liftoff my generator failed, so I pulled the handle to deploy the RAT. It popped out and restored minimal electrical power, enough to talk on the radio. I called my flight leader, Slade Brewer, and said, "I have a generator failure, so I'm going to turn downwind and land. Is everything OK?" He said, "OK. I'm looking for ya, but I don't have ya."

As I entered downwind, the airplane started to roll to the left, so I corrected it with the aileron—no problem. What I didn't know was that I was on fire. The ram air turbine (which supplies power minimum electrical power to communicate and trim the aircraft) is cable-actuated and spring loaded. When you deploy it, you pull the cable to unhook the spring, which lets the turbine pop out. The cable that actuates it runs right next to a wire bundle by your right foot. Although the cable and wire might have been rubbing for years, eventually the friction caused by releasing the cable is enough to fray wires in the bundle and start a small electrical fire. The fire that started on my plane short-circuited the autopilot, which then sent faulty indications to the control system. So the aircraft rolled left again and I corrected it with the aileron and rudder. The plane rolled again and I pushed full aileron and rudder, but it kept rolling.

I thought to myself, "I've got to get out of here. Do I wait until it rolls all the way around so I'm upright, or do I go now?" You want to eject upright, especially when you're that low. Normally you have two ways to eject. If you have time, the primary method of ejection requires reaching for a face curtain and pulling it over your face. This gives you wind-blast protection and gives you better body position—sitting straight up—and you have a better chance of avoiding injury. The secondary method is simply pulling a handle between your legs. Although it's quicker, it doesn't always give you good body position.

But my right foot and right arm were fully extended, operating the aileron and rudder. I had bad body position, and there was no way I could reach the face curtain. So I took the alternate handle between my legs. I moved it three-quarters of an inch, the canopy ejected, and in one and a half seconds I had a full parachute canopy. By then, the airplane had rolled and I was inverted. I was about 500 feet above the water when it spit me out. I remember to this day looking between my feet and seeing nothing but blue sky and an airplane. I remember thinking to myself, "How are you going to explain this one?" That's because I was always pushing the trouble envelope.

I hit the water at about a 40-degree angle. But during that swing, I was able to manually deploy the seat pack—the survival gear. We carried fresh water, pencil flares, bigger flares, a first-aid kit, a pistol, bullets, and a knife. I was wearing a Nomex flight suit and gloves, a helmet, oxygen mask, and boots with steel soles and toes, so I was heavy. I was thinking, "I hope my life preserver doesn't spring an air leak."

I hit the water a couple of miles from the beach, and the airplane crashed right next to me. So I was sitting there in the water with my life preserver on as I watched the plane sink below the waves. I deployed my raft, and I got into it okay, which isn't easy. A rescue helicopter already was out there. I was trained to get out a flare when the helicopter is overhead so they can tell the wind direction. I also was trained to get out of the raft because the rotor wash will pick up the raft into its blades. So I got out of the raft and pushed it away from me. I began trying to light a flare but it wouldn't ignite, which was good, because I had been carrying two 500-pound cans of napalm on the airplane. When the plane hit the water, those thin aluminum cans burst, and numerous chunks of jelly were floating all around me. If napalm ignites, you can't put it out.

Napalm is 46 percent polystyrene (a type of plastic), 33 percent gasoline and 21 percent benzene (a compound similar to gasoline, made from crude oil and coal.) It was named nearly 60 years ago, when scientists from Harvard University and the U.S. Army mixed a soap powder of naphthalene and palmitate with gasoline, fashioning a syrupy material that burns more slowly than gasoline. It can get so hot—routinely more than 5,000 degrees—that it sucks oxygen out of the air and can asphyxiate people even though they may not get burned by it. Napalm was used in Korea to some extent, but it wasn't until the Vietnam War that napalm became known as one of the most fearsome weapons used by U.S. forces.

Next I saw a Marine CH-53 helicopter circling far overhead, but the pilot wouldn't pick me up. I radioed my A-4 buddy Gary, who also was circling overhead, and I said, "Gary, tell these guys if they want to log flight time, do it after they pick me up." What I didn't realize is that particular helicopter can't pick up a person in the water because the rotor wash creates so much turbulence that drowning is likely.

So I sat in the water for about half an hour. Then I saw a Japan Self-Defense Force CH-46 helicopter flying overhead. It was much smaller than the Marines' CH-53. It had a bubble that the crew member could look down through. I remember seeing a crew member looking down at me with great concern on his face. Then they dropped a big horse collar and I knew to let it drop to the water before touching it because static electricity could shock your brains out. I got one arm around the horse collar and they started pulling me up too fast. I lost my grip and dropped about 10 feet back into the water. Then they dropped it again with a whole lot of additional cable to give me plenty of time to get in. I did, but the cable was wrapped around my feet. They pulled me up, but I was upside down and again I fell about 10 feet back into the water. By then I said, "Christ! Maybe I'll just walk to shore." After they dropped it a third time, I managed to hang on and was pulled up into the helicopter.

None of the guys on board spoke English. There I was sitting on the floor of the chopper looking forward, and this guy came back to see me. He was wearing a uniform with pressed trousers, and he put out his hand and shook mine. He mumbled something in Japanese, and I looked behind him and noticed that nobody was flying the helicopter. He was the pilot. I said, "Go back, go back and fly the helicopter!"

I was greatly relieved when the helicopter dropped me off at our base, and I immediately went into the flight surgeon's office and began to tell him what happened. He said, "Just a minute, just a minute!" and he proceeded to pour me a drink. I was still in my wet flight suit and wet boots, so he sent one of his corpsmen to get me a dry flight suit. I still didn't have any dry shoes, so I took off my shoes and socks, and he poured me another drink. He looked at his watch, and said, "It's lunch time, let's go get some lunch." I said, "yes, sir!" We went down to the officers' club on Okinawa called the Four-Forty Club, and they didn't want to let me in because I didn't have any shoes on. The flight surgeon got angry at them and said, "You'd better let him in or we're going to have real trouble here." So we walked right past the maitre d' and sat down to have lunch.

That was about the extent of the medical interview. The only injury that I noticed at the time was bruising in my shoulders from poor body position during ejection. In 1991, orthopedic surgeon Jerry Wilkes, a friend of mine who had been a Navy surgeon, said, "The reason we're operating on your back today is probably due to your ejection 20 years ago."

The Four-Forty Club was made up of three Quonset huts, butted together with cinder block patios between them. It was very functional—not very fancy, but functional. Between the officers' club and the BOQ (bachelor officers' quarters) there was a swamp, and you had to take a taxi to the officers' club to get around the swamp. Occasionally guys would get drunk and try to walk across that swamp. We'd see them about three days later.

The sea water was crystal clear in the Philippines. You'd jump in and think it was about 10 feet deep, but it was actually about 60 feet deep. You wouldn't be able to touch bottom. Flying was great there, too. It was like flying in the Twilight Zone. We'd fly down in these deep canyons and see villagers and grass huts, and they'd never seen an airplane before—much less seeing one go through there at 400 knots per hour. I often wondered, "What are they thinking? Who do they think we are down in this canyon with this big silver bird?" It was so primitive. We dreaded the possibility of being forced down, because we were warned that there were still headhunters in the southern Philippines.

There's a big volcano called Taal Volcano on the island of Luzon, south of the Philippines' capital, Manila. It's now one of the most visited tourist spots in the Philippines. This geological phenomenon is actually a volcano within a lake within a volcano, and we'd fly into the crater and circle the inside.

One Sunday morning two of us went out flying and buzzed Corregidor real low, fast and noisy. We got back to base a couple of hours later and our commanding officer met us out there and said, "Where have you guys been flying?" I said, "We went south." He said, "We've got a reward posted for two guys who flew over Corregidor this morning because that's Ferdinand Marcos' weekend home. He's looking for those two guys." I said, "That wasn't us!" We had flown over his place at about 100 feet having a ball (actually we had flown much lower, but didn't want to get in trouble). I think his wife was down there counting her shoes, while he was counting his money.

I have many fond memories of my time in the Philippines. During my West Pac tour, I remember staying in a barracks called the Mau Camp. We'd go to town every night and get a few beers—San Miguel was about 6 cents a bottle, but they charged us a buck. Back at the Mau Camp, we'd use this urinal, which was a long trench with water running through it. So I was standing there relieving myself, and I looked over and there was this 3-foot hairy animal, which we called a stone ape, standing next to me doing the same thing, except he got a drink when he was finished. I also remember sitting behind the bachelor officers' quarters eating potato chips, with all of these stone apes staring at me. So I tossed the bag down to them, one would pick up the bag and all of his clan would come out and he would pass out potato chips to all of them. It was a sight!

After my West Pac tour ended in 1974, I returned to El Toro and checked in at headquarters and maintenance squadron 13 (H&MS 13). I had obtained a test pilot endorsement at West Pac, so I could become a maintenance test pilot. The second day back, I was scheduled for a 4 p.m. test flight, but one of the senior pilots took my test flight position and made me wait for the next test flight. The senior pilot, with an enlisted man in the back seat, took off and turned downwind. He had trouble with the airplane and ejected off the end of the runway. If that would have been me, I would have ejected during two consecutive flights. A real quirk of fate! The enlisted man had no choice, and he got a super ride! After they ejected, the airplane kept circling over the housing area at about 2,000 feet until it finally crashed in the hills.

Over the next few months, I flew a lot of air combat maneuvering flights for other squadrons, and was discharged from the Marines for good in June 1975.

Chapter 4

Fighting Fires From the Air

When I was a flight instructor at Fullerton Airport, taking students on dual cross-country flights, I often would see columns of smoke from brush fires in the rural and foothill areas that surround the Los Angeles basin. Watching fire bombers became an exciting treat. I'd see TBMs (World War II torpedo bombers) that had been painted a reddish-orange color and adapted to work fires. Back in the mid-1950s, formations of TBMs would fly over our house in Gardena, and my dad would point them out, calling them Turkeys.

After completing active duty with the Marine Corps, I had to figure out how to earn a living. I still wanted to fly but I saw opportunity in the Southern California real estate market. I took a course in real estate sales and obtained my broker's license and sold real estate during the winter. With my Marine Corps credentials, I also applied for and got a job flying fire bombers during the summer of 1975. Flying fire bombers was a seven-day-a-week job during the summer fire season. I was hired by Hemet Valley Flying Service, which was one of about four fire bomber companies in California during the 1960s and 1970s. Their fleet consisted of C-119 "flying boxcars" and S2F "stoofs." We had contracts from the federal Bureau of Land Management, U.S. Forest Service, and the California Department of Forestry. I was trained at our home base in Hemet and at a training facility in Stockton. I started off as an air coordinator (AirCo)—a position that's now called an air attack pilot.

I was assigned to Grass Valley, California. "But where is Grass Valley?" I asked. The chief pilot opened a sectional chart and pointed to a small airport and town in the Northern California gold rush area. After a couple days of training, I was told to be ready to report to Grass Valley on July 1.

Flying an AirCo Cessna 182 certainly was not the S2F that I had wanted to fly, but it was a start. The TBMs had been retired a couple years prior in favor of the twin-engine S2Fs. The Grass Valley area in the Sierra Nevada is a beautiful place about 2,500 feet above sea level with thick green pine forests and more history than I could absorb. According to Gold Country lore, Lyman Gilmore flew a powered aircraft at Gilmore Flying Field months prior to the Wright Brothers' flight at Kitty Hawk. At that location now is Lyman Gilmore Elementary School, which has a wind sock, a monument dedicated to the achievements of Lyman Gilmore, and painted murals on the school buildings showing antique flying machines. The Gold Country is so rich with history.

By the conclusion of my first fire season, I had flown more than 200 hours and was hooked on the fire fighting industry. The following summer found me 120 miles south in another Gold Rush town, Columbia. Still the S2 eluded me, but I had upgraded to a twin-engine Cessna O2A Skymaster. That year the three-month season was extended a month due to dry conditions, and I flew about 300 hours.

Finally, during my third year I went to Pocatello, Idaho, as a copilot in a PBY Catalina fire bomber. This proved to be adventurous because the PBY was under-powered and designed for sea-level operation.

PBY Catalina firebombing on Pocatello, Idaho's west bank

Consequently it was very slow operating at a field elevation of about 4,300 feet above sea level. Hemet Valley Flying Service had two "super boats" powered by Wright R2600s that carried 1,200 gallons of retardant and were used as "scoopers." But not ol' Tanker 83. We had the original Pratt & Whitney 1830-92s, which were underpowered for that altitude, and carried 800 gallons of retardant. A long runway was always a happy sight!

A friendship that will last forever was created when I met PBY Captain Walt Darran. Walt, a former Navy A-1 Skyraider pilot, and I got along quite well, always needling each other about our military backgrounds. For example, I told Walt he could have flown jets if he could think faster. I found it a full-time job trying to keep a sailor in line. We flew only about 30 hours, but it was a great summer.

I remember Walt saying, "This is a strange industry. The captains are reluctant to train their copilots because they think they are training their replacements." But Walt had a different attitude. He said, "You'll never be as good as I am, so I'll teach you everything I know." True to his word, by the end of summer I had a PBY type rating and a U.S. Forest Service Initial Attack rating. I still needle Walt about him saying that I will never be as good as he is. In actuality, I tell him he'll never be as good as I am.

In those days we carried either Fire-Trol or Phos-Chek. It was a red-colored chemical fire retardant with fertilizer properties, so it not only put out the fire, but it also rejuvenated plant growth. Borate was the stuff they first started dropping in the 1950s, and it would put the fire out like gangbusters, but it would sterilize the ground. That's why they switched to Fire-Trol or Phos-Chek.

In 1978, Walt left for other adventures and I had my first air tanker seat as captain of the PBY. My co-pilot, Gale Eaton, and I flew about 50 hours on fires that year. High-altitude airports such as Cody and Rock Springs, Wyoming, and Grand Junction, Colorado, were always a challenge. I remember one particular day in Cody. We had just taken on fuel—the minimum fuel load because of the altitude and temperature. On takeoff as we established a positive rate of climb, up came the gear. We were certainly not a rocket ship and required lots of runway to get off the ground. All of a sudden I heard Gale say, "Have you ever seen an antelope close up? You better turn left or were going to hit one!" Ah, the excitement of fire bombers!

The following year Gale and I both upgraded to the Grumman S-2. Sadly, Gale was killed flying a fire bomber out of Chico, California. I have lost more friends flying fire bombers than in Vietnam.

All of the aircraft used in fire bombing are modified with additional tanks to hold fire retardant material. In those days, the Grumman S-2 held 800 gallons in four 200-gallon tanks, so we could make four 200-gallon drops. If the California Department of Forestry pilot of the air tanker was initial-attack qualified, he could direct his own drops. We would be about 200 feet above the treetops and flying anywhere from 110 to 140 knots, depending upon aircraft, terrain, and local conditions.

Fire creates turbulence, and once we dropped the load, we were not always sure exactly where the turbulence was going to bounce us. I've had fire retardant cover my windshield because the wind turbulence picked it up and threw it in front of me. It was a great job, though. It was like being an ambulance driver who didn't have to obey red

Mike in a PBY Catalina fire bomber

lights anymore. Because of the emergency conditions, flight rules didn't apply.

The last year I flew fire bombers, I was piloting a Grumman S-2 out of the Ramona Air Attack Base in California. I came off a drop late in the day and was heading back empty to Ramona. I was relaxed and thinking I should probably balance my checkbook, when I heard a big loud BANG. I saw the needle for the oil pressure on the right engine drop real quick. So I visually checked the engines and shut down the right engine. But I was at low altitude, and I would have needed another 2,000 feet to clear the tops of a mountain ridge to get back to Ramona. Instead, I pushed the power up on the remaining engine and made a left turn to land at Miramar Naval Air Station. I thought, "It's Friday and almost happy hour," so I contacted the Miramar tower on the emergency frequency and said, "This is tanker 70. You have a localizer frequency?" Naval aviators don't use the term "localizer frequency"—only a civilian or non-Navy pilot would ask for that frequency. The guy in the tower came back with "Roger, 108.9, be advised this is a Naval Air Station." I said, "Roger," and kept tracking on an intercept course. Then I said, "Tanker 70. I'm about eight miles on final. Intercepting the localizer." They said, "Be advised this is a Naval facility." I said, "Roger. I'm six miles on final." They said, "Roger. Be advised this is a Naval facility." I said the magic words, "It's an emergency! I'm going to land." They said, "You're clear to land."

So I landed, and I must have dumped 12 gallons of oil all over the runway. I remember seeing these F-14s shooting "touch-and-goes" and imagining them hitting my oil slick and ricocheting off the runway. I was able to taxi off the runway with the good engine and then shut it down as I arrived in the transit parking area.

In those days, I flew the airplane with cutoff jeans, sandals, long hair and a military helmet. Of course, when I was sitting in the airplane, people on the ground couldn't see I wasn't wearing a flight suit. All they could see was a guy in a helmet. So I parked the airplane and three military police (MPs) came out to meet me. They saw that I was wearing a military helmet, flying a former military airplane that was painted a funny fire bomber green color. They didn't know what to think. So I got out of the cockpit, walked to the midsection and jumped out of the airplane. I took off my helmet, and I was standing there with no shirt and hair down to my shoulders. We began a terse exchange. They asked, "Where's the pilot?" I said, "I'm the pilot." They asked, "What are you doing?"

I said, "I had an engine out, and I had to land here." They asked, "What do you do?" I said, "I fly airplanes."

Just then I noticed three TA-4s entering the break overhead. They came in and parked right next to me on the transit line. I told the MP, "I probably know those guys." I don't think they believed me, but just then three pilots with three students from VT-22 training command got out of the airplane and they waved at me, yelling, "Mike, how are ya doin', I haven't seen you in a long time." The MPs were probably thinking, "Who is this masked man?" Well, I knew those pilots from when I was on active duty. So they came over and rescued me from the MPs. We went to the Officers' Club that night and had an enjoyable time.

I was out there the next morning at 8 a.m. starting to remove the engine when my boss from Hemet Valley Flying Service called and asked, "What are you doing?" I said, "I've got the engine ready to come off—did you get me a new engine?" He said, "We won't have an engine for two weeks." Frustrated, I put all the parts in a pile and went home for two weeks. The mechanics from Hemet Valley Flying Service finished it up, and I flew it home from there. I flew two more fires, and that was the end of my fire-fighting career.

Chapter 5

Flying in South America

In addition to selling real estate during the winter months, and flying fire bombers during the summer, I found several oddball flying jobs. I was driving up Lakewood Boulevard toward my mother's house in Long Beach one day in 1978, probably to borrow some money from her—sons never change—when I drove by Long Beach Airport. Sitting there was a PBY similar to the one I flew in Pocatello, Idaho, except it had been modified. I stopped to look and noticed it had been upgraded to Pratt & Whitney 1830-94 engines with a boat under each wing. It also had clear bubbles for viewing and an aft air stair door. It also had two additional engines—Lycoming GSO-480s with reversible three-bladed propellers. I thought, "Mmm, a strange four-engine airplane." That particular PBY was made in Palm Springs by a Dr. Forrest Bird in the late 1960s, and they called it the Bird Flying Boat. His idea was to tour the world with his "flying hospital." The airplane was white with a red cross painted on the tail, and it had sterilization ovens, operating areas, and oxygen piped throughout the airplane.

Picking out an individual who seemed to be in charge, I asked, "You guys need any pilots?" He said, "Yeah. Have you ever flown one of these?" I said, "Yeah, I have, and I'm type-rated and current on PBYs," which was rare. So they took my name and phone number and explained, "We're going to need some pilots, because we're going to South America with the airplane on a research project." About a week later, they called me and said, "We have an opening for a third pilot-mechanic." I said, "I'm sorry, that doesn't interest me. I'm a captain." They said, "Well, you can't start at the top." I said, "Well then, I can't start at all." About a week later they called back and said, "Do you want to go as co-captain?" I said, "Yeah, I'll go." The salary for the job was $1,000 per week, all expenses paid.

The South America research project was funded by a Department of the Interior contract. Six scientists from Scripps Institution of Oceanography were on board the airplane when we took off. From Long Beach, we flew to San Diego, then to Puerto Vallarta, Tapachula, Mexico, Guatemala City, Costa Rica, Ecuador, and went as far as Lima, Peru. Our goal was to go 800 miles out to sea every other day at 500 feet on a search pattern. The researchers were tracking the dolphin population between Long Beach and Lima, Peru. We were going to take that whole survey into the South Pacific, but we never got that far.

When we were in Tapachula, Mexico, which is walking distance to the Guatemala border, we heard that a lot of pyramids were in the area. So we went across into Guatemala to see them, and we met this little kid on the highway. We asked him where the pyramids were and he told us to park our car and come with him. He said, "I show you pyramids." He took us over hill, over dale, over streams and we finally got to see the pyramids. They were fascinating. After we had spent some time exploring, the kid said, "Now you come to my village." Nervously we followed him along a roundabout path to his village, and he introduced us to his mother, who brought out a guest book for us to sign. We gave him some money and he took us to our cars, which were only about 100 yards away. He was a little con man who had taken us on a circuitous wild goose chase to make us lose track of where we had parked our cars!

They had these giant iguanas down there and the villagers captured them for food. Iguanas even slept on the roof of our hotel. The villagers would carry these four-foot iguanas that must have weighed about 80 pounds apiece on a pole, and they sold them at the marketplace for food.

The airport at Tapachula had a control tower, and we bought oil and gas there for the PBY. The aircraft had a capacity of 65 gallons of oil per engine, and it was common for us to buy 20 to 30 gallons of oil at a stop. We bought 30 gallons of oil there, and they brought it to us in one-quart cans. We developed a very efficient operation—we had a guy on the ground, and he would toss the oil can up to the catcher on the wing. The guy on the wing would open it with a church key, and hand it to a guy who would pour it into the oil tank. That guy would toss the empty can to another guy on the ground. While we were filling up, the American Bonanza Society, an organization of small-aircraft pilots came through on a tour. The first guy landed and told the tower controller to go take a siesta. The controller obliged, allowing the pilot to run the tower so he could talk in English to the 20 airplanes coming in. Every day was different.

I spent a whole winter with that survey group, and figured that was the last I would see of Latin America. I was wrong.

When I returned to California, I had gone back to work for Hemet Valley Flying Service flying fire bombers. During the winter, one of my pilot buddies there, Bob Forbes, asked, "You were down in Central America last winter, weren't you?" I said, "Yeah." He asked, "You know how to get through customs, don't you? Do you know how to speak Spanish?" I said, "I know enough." He said, "You want to go down to South America for a job? It pays $1,000 per week, it's legal and all expenses are paid." I said, "Okay." But I didn't even ask him what it was. He said, "Meet me at the company Christmas party." So we were sitting there at the 1978 Christmas party and I said, "Bob, you didn't tell me what we're going to be doing in South America." He said, "We're gonna go to Honduras and fly Corsairs." The Corsairs had been the former first-line fighters for the Honduran Air Force.

So the next day, Bob and I left Hemet and drove down to Los Angeles International Airport, met two other guys, and flew to New Orleans, where we picked up two more pilots. We left New Orleans on a SAHSA Airlines 737 headed for Tegucigalpa, the capital of Honduras. So there we were, six travelers with Levis, tennis shoes and helmet bags on the airplane—trying to

Members of the Honduran Corsair mission: from left, Lou Remschner, pilot (died in a C-119 fire bomber about 1985); Howard Pardue, purchased the Corsairs with Robert Ferguson; Mike Penketh, pilot; Harold Beale, pilot; Bob Forbes, pilot; Ed Real, pilot (died in an S-2 fire bomber about 1990); Robert Ferguson, partner of Howard Pardue; Jim, who initially put the deal together for Pardue and Ferguson; missing: Orrin Carr, pilot (died about 1990).

act inconspicuous. We had one handbook on the Corsair that was written in English. Ed Real read the book and he told us about the airplanes. That was our ground school.

As we were en route to Tegucigalpa, the captain came back to talk to us. He had on a white shirt and embroidered wings, and his name tag said "Captain Fernando Soto." Although this was not a secret or clandestine operation in any way, we had been told that we should not discuss our reason for being there. Captain Soto was talking to us about Honduras and just shooting the breeze, and then he started walking to the cockpit and turned around and said, "You guys will like the Corsairs." Some secret! He knew all about it!

When we arrived at Tegucigalpa, we saw eight F4U Corsairs, sitting in grass about two feet tall. It was a beautiful sight! They were combat airplanes, equipped with gun sights, rocket racks and armor plating. They were not like the Reno air racing Corsairs that we see today. One airplane had been kept on a pedestal in front of base operations as a monument because it had been flown by the only ace in South American history. He had shot down two Mustangs and a Corsair during the Soccer War between Honduras and El Salvador. When we got close enough to look at that airplane, we saw that the ace's name was written on the fuselage beneath the cockpit. I'll be damned if it wasn't "Captain Fernando Soto."

We learned that two Americans had bought the entire Corsair Air Force from Honduras. They're worth about $1.5 million apiece today, but they probably paid $75,000 for each. They hired us to fly them to California so they could sell them for a profit. Most of the Corsairs were built after World War II. The one I flew actually saw combat in the Korean War with U.S. Navy fighter squadron VF-92.

After our first Corsair flight in Tegucigalpa, we were welcomed upon landing by what appeared to be the entire town. We weren't sure if they had come to say goodbye to the Corsairs that saved their country during the Soccer War, or if they thought they were at war again.

We spent about two weeks in Honduras because of delays, but they provided rooms and meals for us, and we got to fly the airplanes several times before we left. None of us had ever flown a Corsair before, so we conducted self check-outs, what a thrill. We had one manual written in English, the rest were in Spanish. Fellow pilot Ed Real read the English version and told us everything we should know.

We spent about a week flying the Corsairs in Tegucigalpa before proceeding northbound to the United States.

On our way to Houston, Texas, we stopped for lunch in Mexico. After eating a bacon, lettuce and tomato sandwich I eventually became deathly ill. Tomatoes and lettuce are grown on the ground, and I quickly learned that in that region you should never eat any produce that touches the ground because of fertilizers and unsanitary conditions. I later had to give up my airplane in Harlingen, Texas (just across the Mexican border), while I recovered.

Although my experience with Corsairs was short-lived, it marked the completion of a circle in my life. My father had been in VMF-214 with Corsairs during the Korean Conflict, I was in VMA-214 flying A-4s, and I wound up in Honduras flying my dad's old Corsairs. My journeys from Korea to El Toro to Honduras had sent me on a fulfilling orbit. It was a tremendous adventure. I was sitting in the cockpit of the World War II airplane on which my father had worked.

Chapter 6

My Introduction to Aerobatics

When I worked for Aviation Unlimited at Fullerton Airport in the winter of 1965, an owner of one of the lease-back airplanes there had a Citabria, which is basically an Aeronca aerobatic airplane. It was one of the very first 7ECA Citabrias with a 100-horsepower Continental engine. The owner of the airplane took me up twice to show me how to do aerobatics—loops, rolls, spins, and split-S maneuvers. That was the extent of my aerobatics training.

One day, the chief pilot said, "Mike, I just signed up a guy for an aerobatic course and you're our only aerobatic instructor." Two times up and I'm an instructor!

My student was a California Highway Patrol officer who had bought a 10-hour aerobatic course. We went out and taught each other how to do aerobatics, and that's how I learned aerobatics. I've always been so comfortable in an airplane—I've never been afraid.

The experiences teaching (and learning) aerobatics prompted me to buy my first Pitts aerobatic airplane in 1976. I traded my second Corvette, a 1964 model that I had bought in 1973, plus cash for the Pitts. The Pitts is like no other airplane in the world. It is so light and so responsive, and it's extremely fast relative to its size. I have a friend named Ken Cox who had a Starduster Too, an amateur-built biplane, and he took me up in that a few times for practice before my first flight in the Pitts.

The directional control of the Pitts can be very demanding because it has a short fuselage and it tends to zigzag down the runway. A lot of spectators watched my first takeoff at Compton Airport, and I used the entire width but only about 500 feet of the length of the runway. I took off and I had to fly back to Corona Municipal Airport, where I had a hangar. So I did aerobatics for about half an hour and I thought, "I may be running out of gas. I guess I've gotta land this thing now." Landing a Pitts can be challenging, too, but I landed it okay. It's a superb aerobatic airplane—it's so much fun!

A good friend of mine, Audie Searcy, was a chief pilot for a company in Costa Mesa called Computer Automation. The owner had a Beechcraft Duke, and Audie flew that for them. After the owner went out and bought a Pitts S2A, a two-seat airplane, Audie called me up and said, "Mike, we just bought an S2A Pitts and nobody here knows how to fly it. Will you check me out in it?" So there I went again. I was teaching someone to fly a two-seater Pitts that I had never flown in my life. We picked up the airplane at Riverside's Flabob Airport, which had a very short runway. And there I taught Audie and his boss how to fly the airplane.

The summer after I had bought my first Pitts, my fire bombing job took me to Columbia Air Attack Base in Columbia, California. At the end of the runway was a hangar owned by a man named Joe Pfeifer, who was well known in the aviation world. He specialized in World War I antique restorations, and he built some of the airplanes that were flown in the early movies. I got to know Joe really well. He had suffered a disabling stroke and was an ornery, cantankerous old man, but he liked me. I would have coffee with Joe every morning. He would cuss and bitch at me and I always said, "Yessir,

yessir," and we became good friends.

Joe designed the Christian inverted aircraft oil system that is used on all aerobatic airplanes. One day he said to me, "I want you to put an oil system on your Pitts, so you can maintain oil pressure when you fly upside down." So I went out and bought one and he showed me how to install it.

The next summer I was back at Columbia and Joe said, "Mike, why don't you get your A&P [airframe and power plant] license." That license allowed pilots to perform mechanical work on their own aircraft as well as other people's airplanes. He said, "You know I'm an examiner, don't you?" I said, "Yes, I know." He said, "I shouldn't have to say any more then."

So I went out and bought all of the Acme study guides for an airframe and power plant license. There were three tests—general knowledge, airframe and power plant. I took all three tests in Fresno and came back with the results and showed Joe. He looked at the results and said, "Damn! I knew you were smart, but I didn't know you were that smart!" He said, "We'll do your practical test next week." So I got all studied up and went into his office and he said, "Make me a cup of coffee. You're doing good." Then he said, "We'll do the oral. Tell me what Ohm's law is." I said, "Joe, I don't know." He said, "Well, Ohm's law is if you don't get it at home, you go elsewhere." I laughed and he told me the reason he liked me was that I laughed, enjoyed life and airplanes. Then he said, "You're not overwhelmingly qualified in civilian airplane mechanics, but you know enough to know what you don't know, and I trust that you'll always ask or read a book. On the basis of that, I'll give you an A&P license." What a compliment that was! I was qualified to seek employment as a mechanic, but I mainly got the license to work on my own airplane.

Chapter 7

Landing an Airline Job

I had wanted to be a commercial airline pilot since childhood. I started applying to the airlines the day I got out of college. The minimum requirement was to be 18 years old with a commercial instrument rating. But in all practicality, that isn't even close to what it took to get hired. I got turned down many, many times. In reality, they were looking for 3,000 hours flight time with an IFR (instrument flight rules) rating. When I got out of the Marine Corps, I had about 4,500 hours under my belt. Having the experience of flying jet aircraft gave me a competitive edge, so I thought.

I started applying to all the airlines again while I was stationed at Columbia Airport flying fire bombers. The first reply I received was from Hughes Airwest, which sent me a postcard saying, "No thank you," and it had postage due on it. Talk about an insult! I interviewed with Pacific Southwest airlines (PSA) about the same time, but they had misfiled my application within the flight attendant stack, and I found out I was being interviewed for a flight attendant job. I should have pursued that job. I probably would have been hired and gotten my foot in the door.

I was finally hired by AirCal on January 5, 1981. AirCal began as Air California in 1967, operating two turboprop Lockheed L-188 Electras between San Francisco and Orange County. Douglas DC-9s were added to the fleet with Boeing 737-100s and 200s coming along in the early 1970s. The name AirCal was adopted in the 1980s. I initially flew between San Diego and Anchorage, and AirCal later added flights to Chicago and the Midwest.

AirCal recruited high-time pilots—essentially they were hiring captains. But newly hired flight personnel always started as copilots (first officer). The other airlines generally had a three-person crew—pilot, first officer, and flight engineer, so they'd hire a pilot who would spend several years as flight engineer and several more years as first officer, before being upgraded to captain. I became a captain in 1985, only four years after joining AirCal.

New-hire school for any airline takes about three months of total training. AirCal was based in Newport Beach, and ground school there lasted an entire month, followed by about a month of simulator training, actual aircraft flight training, and finally initial operating experience (IOE) training. During the flight training portion, we'd get about three flights in the actual airplane while it was on a layover at Sacramento Metropolitan Airport—usually at midnight or 1 a.m. They'd take an airplane off the line because they weren't using it to make money, and we'd go out and train with it. Our training was done in an empty aircraft—mostly touch-and-go landings. After that we went through observation flights in the jump seat on the airplane, then IOE (initial operating experience), usually with a check airman as captain. The IOE flights were normally scheduled flights with passengers aboard.

One time, during my early days of being a reserve captain, I was called for a flight at Orange County Airport. So I rushed to the airport, jumped into the airplane and

I saw a face I hadn't seen in years. I said, "Colonel Davis, what are you doing here?" He said, "Sit down lieutenant. I've got your flight plan all done for ya." My AirCal first officer was Mike Davis, who had been my A4 instructor in the Marine Corps. At AirCal, the pilot and co-pilot would swap every other landing and takeoff to keep both in practice.

I didn't have a fixed route. We didn't bid for routes; we'd bid for days off. Airline people don't have weekends—all the days are the same. It worked out to be about 15 days on, 15 off. I drove from my home near Auburn to San Francisco, Oakland or San Jose. When I was on reserve, I had to be within an hour of the airport at all times. After a couple of years, I had enough seniority to hold a regular line. I bought a Beech Debonair to fly from my home in Auburn, California, to work in San Jose and Oakland.

Some of the more challenging airports were Reno, because of the altitude, winds and weather, and South Lake Tahoe, where because of altitude and terrain only the later-model Boeing 737-300 was allowed to fly. Pilots were required to have a special qualification to fly in and out of South Lake Tahoe, which is situated in a blind canyon and necessitated straight-in or downwind south landing patterns. The extremely high altitude, resulting in thin air, can present challenging conditions for maneuvering in that canyon. I thought it was fun. Landing at San Diego was always a kick because we came in at a steep approach over downtown San Diego. You could actually see into the buildings on short final. Burbank had a very short runway. You had to be right on your speeds—there's no room for error. "Special qualification" airports, such as South Lake Tahoe and some of the high-altitude airports at ski areas in Colorado, required special familiarization, usually through an FAA video, to operate from those airports.

Today, the art of flying commercial jets with your hands in high-density areas is almost lost—it's all automated. It's become so complex it has to be automated. Flying an airplane without an autopilot is almost an emergency procedure. You are so busy, you need the help of the autopilot as well as the first officer. When I started flying for AirCal, automation was available, but our airplanes had only a basic autopilot compared to the more sophisticated systems available.

AirCal was a great employer and a financially solid airline—so much so that it was bought by American Airlines in 1987.

When I was flying one weekend in an aerobatics contest in the San Joaquin Valley town of Taft, I met a young pilot there who told me he had just been hired by American Airlines, but he had postponed his start date because he wanted to finish school. I said, "You should never postpone a start date, because you might lose 100 numbers of seniority." Seniority is extremely important in the airline industry. It controls the equipment you fly and the base you fly out of, which determines your income. It also controls your family life in that it controls your days off, weekends off, and vacation periods. About three months later, American Airlines called me for a flight out of San Francisco. I walked into the operations room and my first officer was that same kid I had met at the aerobatic contest, and it was among his earliest flights for the airline.

So I took off for Chicago's O'Hare Airport with my new first officer. We knew the weather was bad, and deteriorating. As we approached O'Hare we switched from center (air traffic control) to the approach control. We were told that several flights had missed their approaches, and traffic was starting to back up at the nearby alternate airports. I rechecked our fuel and said to the controller, "If we should miss the approach, we will be requesting immediate vectors to our alternate airport"—in this case, Madison, Wisconsin.

Because of the deteriorating weather we briefed for what is called a Category III auto-land approach, often called a "zero-zero" landing, because there are no ceiling requirements. The only requirement is an RVR (runway visual range) of 600 feet. RVR is the distance measured in feet that pilots can see straight ahead from the cockpit. RVR is measured from three locations: touchdown, midfield and roll-out.

The crew, aircraft, and airport must be individually certified for this type of approach. Many simulator training sessions are made practicing this approach along with the required crew coordination. As a confidence builder we also made auto-lands in VFR (visual flight rules) weather. VFR rules govern the procedures for conducting flight under visual conditions.

A Category III auto-land approach is a fully automated procedure monitored (flown) by the first officer with his hands on the throttle. All the captain does is monitor the approach and make the required verbal calls while looking straight ahead. When the captain sees the airport he simply says, "I've got it." He then lifts the first officer's hands from the throttles, retards the power and completes the landing. The concentration is so intense it's often said, "If the captain were to die on the approach, the first officer would not be aware of it." If the first officer does not hear "I've got it," he is trained to simultaneously rotate the aircraft to a climb attitude and apply climb power, check for a positive rate of climb, retract the landing gear, retract the flaps on schedule, and call in to the tower, "Missed approach." Only then would the first officer realize he or she was flying solo.

Chapter 8

Reno Air Racing

I was going to be single forever—or so I thought—until I met Peggy Gershbach at Ted Heineman's shop in South Santa Ana. Ted was a building contractor, and a pilot, and his shop was two miles from Orange County Airport. Every Friday night for more than 10 years I would meet at Ted's shop with all of my sport airplane buddies. Peggy was a licensed pilot, too. She had three daughters and had lost her husband in an airplane crash several years before I met her. At the time, my daughter, Shelley, who was 9 years old, came to live with me after having a falling out with her mother. I thought living in a household with me and Peggy, and her three daughters would be a good, stable upbringing for Shelley.

After Peggy and I were engaged, we flew my Piper J3 Cub to Northern California from Corona Airport in Southern California. We first went to Cameron Airpark and looked at airport property. Then we went to Grass Valley because I wanted to take her to Friar Tuck's Restaurant in Nevada City. En route to Nevada City, we flew over Lake of the Pines, between Grass Valley and Nevada City. I noticed people water skiing on the lake, and houses were being built along the lake.

We were married in 1983, and bought a 4,000-square-foot newly built home on the lake. We had a ski boat in the backyard, and water skied in the summer and snow skied in the winter. We also had a hangar at Auburn Municipal Airport, about 10 miles down State Highway 49.

In 1984 we formed IAC (International Aerobatic Club) Chapter 73 at Auburn Airport. Peggy was president and I was vice president. We sold the J3 Cub and bought a 1962 Beechcraft Debonair that I used to commute to work in San Jose and Oakland. I also finished building a Pitts S1S for aerobatic competitions and for racing at Reno's Stead Airport.

In 1984 I watched my friend and neighbor Earl Allen race in the biplane class at the National Championship Air Races and Air Show at Stead Air Force Base. The races, which began in 1964, now include six classes of competitions: unlimited, AT-6/SNJ/Harvard, Formula One, biplane, sport, and jet. I competed for the first time in 1985 in Passion Pitts, a biplane Peggy and I had bought after we were married, placing sixth in the Gold category race that year. I raced Passion Pitts at Reno for the next three years, while building a modified, faster, Pitts S1S.

I finished building "My Pitts" S1S in 1988, and qualified for the Gold biplane competition at 187 miles per hour.

When you first qualify to fly the race course, you complete 10 laps, either by yourself or with no more than two other airplanes. In an actual race many times you don't even see the other six airplanes; it's as if you've got the sky to yourself.

As the biplane class president, I would put an instructor pilot out there and told the new competitors to watch him complete a lap or two. "After the new competitor flies and watches one or two laps," I said, "you can move down as low as you feel comfortable and fly with the instructor pilot for a couple of laps. Then, he may pull power back and slip behind you, and you go fly the course. He may pass you, so you can have the experience of seeing an airplane pass because that can really get your attention." It takes a speed differential of only about five miles an hour to pass another airplane. As a student, I was told, "Never pass inside another airplane, unless it's going really wide. Never pass below another airplane, unless it's going really high."

Consistency is very important. I always encouraged biplane competitors to, "fly an aggressive course, but fly a safe course." I'd say, "Pay attention to the airplane in front of you. What kind of airplane is it? What kind of prop does it have? Does that mean it accelerates fast or slow on the runway?" I'd walk around the race pit area and talk to every pilot, every day of the races. I was checking their mental attitude for indications of complacency, overconfidence, insecurity, nervousness, or apprehension.

Three different speed groups (Bronze, Silver, Gold) were determined by heat races. Racers qualified Monday, Tuesday or Wednesday, and the heat races were on Thursday. Bronze medal event competitors raced on Friday, Silver competitors raced on Saturday, and Gold competitors raced on Sunday. These rules go back to the mid-1980s, and they may have changed since my last race in 1993.

On September 18, 1993, I won first in the Silver Biplane Class, with a speed of 182.098 miles per hour. It would be the last time I would race at Reno.

Mike with Mary Ann Harr and our sponsor Bernie Fox at Reno Air Races in 1991 (photo by Marti Smiley Childs)

Chapter 9

A Grinding Crash

I met Mary Ann Harr in 1981. She was a flight attendant for AirCal and she had a "significant other" at the time. We enjoyed flying together and remained good friends at the airlines, but we always seemed to be out of phase—I was married when she was dating, then she had a significant other when I was available. We were finally in sync in 1989, and I'll never forget our first date.

I was talking on the phone with her and after I hung up, AirCal's scheduling department called and assigned me to a trip that included all day off in Las Vegas. The next day was my birthday, so I called Mary Ann back and asked her to meet me in Las Vegas. She was off that day, so she was able to "dead-head"—she took a space-available flight—over to Las Vegas from Burbank (now called Bob Hope Airport).

I walked into the hotel lobby the next day in Las Vegas with my entire flight crew (three flight attendants and copilot) and we checked in. The receptionist at the front desk said, "Captain Pen-

Mike Penketh and his wife, Mary Ann Harr, in their American Airlines uniforms

keth, a woman has already checked into your room." Of course, we were supposed to be on the sly, but everyone laughed. There was Mary Ann hanging out by the pool with a magazine covering her face. But her cover got blown quickly. All of the cards fell into place.

I don't like being alone. I like having a partner in life, and Mary Ann fit all of my ideals. She was smart, pleasant, slim, pretty and had a great job. My life was mostly set because an airline captain makes fairly good money. I was looking forward to being a captain for 20 years, and I wanted someone to share that with. I think we were both looking for companionship and security. It was great that both of us were airline employees, because we could travel together wherever we wanted to, on the spur of the moment. We'd take off to the Caribbean for a week, or St. Thomas, St. John's, Antigua, Grenada, or the Florida Keys. At that time, airline employees worked about 15 days a month and got five days off in a row, which meant monthly mini vacations for us.

After my marriage to Peggy was dissolved and the judge told me to leave Lake of the Pines, I moved into a dumpy little apartment in Vacaville, along Interstate 80 between Sacramento and the San Francisco Bay Area. After about nine months in the apartment, I bought a new two-bedroom, two-bath house in the Vacaville hills. I was able to get a 50- by 40-square-foot hangar at Nut Tree Airport, about 10 minutes from home. Both my Pitts S1S, and the 1962 Beechcraft Debonair that I had bought in 1988 to commute from Auburn to work in San Jose and Oakland, fit in the hangar. Mary Ann lived in Garden Grove, which is not far from Long Beach Airport, and I frequently flew there in the Debonair from Vacaville.

I chose the Debonair because it was relatively inexpensive, relatively fast, and well equipped. It was an IFR (instrument-rated) airplane. When my divorce finalized, Mary Ann and I moved in together, and then we bought a bigger house farther up the street in Vacaville. We had a comfortable life—both working for American Airlines and bidding time off to travel together. We made lots of friends in our neighborhood and we went everywhere together, including aerobatics competitions, the annual Reno Air Races and land speed racing at Bonneville.

I went to Fort Collins, Colorado, to have an airplane engine rebuilt for my Pitts S1S by an aircraft engine builder who also enjoyed hot rods. He had a fiberglass-

Mike and Mary Ann on a tour of the Queen Mary in Long Beach, CA. (photo by Marti Smiley Childs)

body replica of a Ford Cobra sitting in his shop. Cobras came out in 1963, and they were built at Los Angeles International Airport. It's a little two-seat road racer capable of going about 200 mph. I just wanted it for street use. Carroll Shelby had a showroom on Sepulveda Boulevard, and I used to go down there when I was in high school and sit in Cobras. In those days, you could buy a Cobra for about $3,800. Now they're about a half-million dollars. Eventually, I wound up buying the Ford Cobra kit car from Dick DeMars in Colorado.

Then I became involved with construction of a Reno Unlimited-category air racer with my friend Gary Childs. I reacquainted myself with all of my auto racing buddies in Whittier, California, to build a high-performance, aluminum auto engine for our race plane. That's when I met Leonard Carr, a very experienced (and fast) Bonneville racer, who owns Champion Performance in Whittier. I said to Leonard, "I'll give you the Cobra to sell, and we'll use that money to build a Bonneville race car." Leonard sold the Cobra for $10,000 to a gentleman in Whittier.

Leonard found a guy in Corona who wanted to sell a rear-engine dragster chassis he had built, so we bought it and modified it into a Lakester for Bonneville racing.

Our Lakester was an open-wheel, rear-engine car, and we stretched the wheel base to about 225 inches, hoping to increase stability.

Mary Ann and I had visited Leonard at the Bonneville races in 1991 and 1992, flying the Debonair to Wendover Airport, the closest public airport to the Bonneville salt flats. It was a historically fascinating place where B29 Cruiser crews were trained to drop the atom bombs on Hiroshima and Nagasaki. To this day huge hangars with thousands of little 12-inch square window panes still exist there. It's deathly quiet at night, and it's so spooky knowing that's where the crew for the Enola Gay trained in 1945.

After winning the silver race at Reno on Saturday and celebrating my victory with Mary Ann and my friends and fellow racers on Sunday, I flew My Pitts from Reno to Nut Tree Airport in Vacaville on Monday morning, September 20, 1993. I quickly re-packed some clothes, climbed into the Debonair, took off, and arrived at Bonneville late that afternoon. I was excited to see just how fast the Lakester that Leonard had been working on for the past two years would fly across the salt flats.

Bonneville racers lined up for a run in 1990 (photo by Marti Smiley Childs)

The Bonneville Salt Flats is an area of barren land that covers more than 30,000 acres. During the ice age it was approximately the size of Lake Michigan, but it's somewhat smaller today. It's been said that the Bonneville Salt Flats is so featureless that you can almost see the curvature of the earth there.

The surface of the salt flats contains potassium, magnesium, lithium, and sodium chloride—common table salt. During the winter, temperatures can dip well below freezing, and a shallow layer of standing water covers most of the surface of the salt flats. Beginning in spring, high temperatures, low humidity and wind slowly evaporate this water, leaving a vast, nearly perfectly flat plain. Water, always present, can form shallow ponds and small lakes overnight—even when the daytime temperatures hover around (and often exceed) the 100-degree mark.

The 1846 Donner Party had great difficulty crossing the salt flats. The Donner Party lost considerable time, along with several oxen and wagons, which delayed their attempt to cross the Sierra Nevada until too late in the summer, resulting in their tragic story. As early as 1896, Bonneville was recognized as a potential race site—not for cars, but for bicycles.

Bonneville land speed records can vary widely among different types of vehicles. The record for a 50cc motorcycle may be less than 100 mph, while the mark for a streamliner vehicle is in excess of 400 mph, and a jet car can top 600 mph. The first unofficial auto speed record was set in 1914 at 141.73 miles per hour. In 1949, Bonneville became popular among speed racing enthusiasts, and by 1970, U.S. racer Gary Gabolich attained a spectacular speed of 622.4 miles per hour in his rocket car called Blue Flame.

Today, speed is associated with the Bonneville Salt Flats, which is among the world's elite land-speed

Mike at Bonneville in 1990—three years prior to the crash that took his hands (photo by Marti Smiley Childs)

trial locales that also include the Black Rock Desert in Northern Nevada, the Muroc and El Mirage dry lakes in Southern California, and Lake Eyre, a large salt lake situated between two deserts in one of Australia's driest regions.

Bonneville race events are divided into two groups: long course and short course. The "short" course is intended for cars under 200 mph. It's a three-mile, straightaway course with a several-mile "shutdown area" to allow the cars to decelerate. The long course is intended for cars exceeding 200 mph, and includes a five-mile straightaway course and a several-mile "shutdown area." On the long course, the cars are timed at the two-mile mark, which in Bonneville lingo is referred to as "the quarter," and the three-, four- and five-mile marks. The "long black line" marking the course continues for several more miles to allow for "shutdown." Drivers can choose either the right or left side of the black line when they begin the speed attempt.

Many classes of cars compete for land speed records, with individual records set in each class. The vehicles include motorcycles, stock (street-driven) cars, antiques, turbine-powered, diesel-powered, electric-powered and specially built cars. Many classes are then subdivided by the type of fuel being used. Gasoline engines use the typical pump gas available from local gas stations. Fuel includes special mixtures of alcohol and nitromethane used in specially built land-speed record cars. Other fuels, such as propane, jet fuel or diesel are used in their respective classes.

To set a speed record at Bonneville, a qualifying run must be faster than the existing record for that class. A return run in the opposite direction must then be completed, and the two-run average must exceed the existing record to establish a new record. Depending on the organization promoting the speed trials, the return

Bonneville 1990 (photo by Marti Smiley Childs)

run is usually made about an hour after the initial run, but sometimes it is made the following morning. Between the runs the car is considered to be in the "impound area," where safety procedures and minor tune-ups can be completed. These minor tune-ups can sometimes be major, depending on the designated impound time. Time is the element, as the return run must be initiated at the starter's command. If the car cannot make the return record run, all effort is wasted. This is where the maintenance crews must determine the time required

119

for the "minor" or "major" mechanical work to be accomplished. Safety items, such as refueling, oil and filter changes, parachute re-packs, or tire changes are paramount during this impound time, as the car must pass a visual safety inspection before the return run is attempted.

All cars begin from a standing start at the start line. Despite their enormous horsepower, these high-performance cars have such high gear ratios that they don't move well on their own from the start. Race teams use a push truck to propel the cars as fast as the truck can go, maybe 70 to 80 miles per hour. The truck driver honks his horn when he's reached his maximum speed and the free ride is over. The race car driver lets out the clutch, and away he goes! It's an incredible feeling!

The actual geographic altitude of the Bonneville salt flats is just over 4,200 feet, but the density altitude is much greater—that is, the warmer the temperature and the higher the elevation, the slower the performance. When tuning a car at sea level, race crews always try to compensate for the density altitude and temperature, but usually final adjustments are made at the race site.

Our race car was called an EF/L (Engine Fuel/ Lakester). The engine was a 307-cubic-inch Chevrolet, destroked to 258 cubic inches. This was to comply with the F class engine requirements of 184 to 260 cubic inches. The fuel was a mixture of alcohol and nitromethane. The car had been originally designed to be a rear-engine dragster, originally with a 207-inch wheelbase, which we lengthened to approximately 225 inches. The 18-inch stretch gave us ample, but not excessive, room for a dry sump oil tank and the necessary drives. Attached to a 2.73:1 geared 9-inch Ford rear end were 33-inch diameter tires. It had a pneumatically controlled three-speed racing transmission built by Lenco Equipment Company in Lemon Grove, California. The transmission was unique in its use of a clutch to engage the engine. From then on, shifts were pneumatically controlled by using a push button.

A Hilborn fuel injection system, aluminum heads with titanium valves, along with every trick in the book completed this engine. The cooler-running alcohol fuel allowed us to use a compression ratio of 13:1. The terribly acrid smell of an alcohol-burning car is like nothing else. It cannot be described—it burns your eyes, and I think it'll eliminate nasal hairs. Fast? You bet! The EF/L class record in 1993 was 263 mph, and our car was capable of a top speed in excess of 300 mph.

On Monday, Leonard worked on the car and made a practice run, or two. I arrived late Monday and prepared for practice runs on Tuesday. The fuel injector has what is called a "pill," which meters the amount of fuel going into the fuel injection system, and you've got to get the right pill—the right fuel/air mixture. The pill is simply a fitting with a metered hole to pass the fuel between the fuel pump and the fuel injectors. The size of this metered hole controls the volume of fuel reaching the cylinders. On several of our runs the car failed to gather enough speed, and I had to terminate by turning off the course early.

By Wednesday afternoon frustration had set in, and we were running out of ideas. As a last resort, Leonard decided to change the pill in the fuel injection. Our next step was to conduct some low-speed test runs, maybe 20 mph maximum, in the practice area. We both smiled at the results, headed back to the pits, and I topped off the alcohol, while wizard Leonard prepared a slight dose of nitro fuel.

Because of alternating long- and short-course cars, our wait for a run was about an hour as we hand-pushed the car toward the start line. Just before racing, I put on a fire-resistant Nomex driving suit and boots. I also wore Nomex socks and long underwear beneath the driving suit. I smiled at Leonard and joked, "kinda roomy, this must be your driving suit!" Although Leonard was physically fit, he was a tad larger than I was. A Nomex hood and gloves follow as the bottoms of the legs and sleeves are tightened with Velcro straps. It was afternoon—maybe one o'clock—and it was getting hot. I put on the full-face helmet. Looking like a man from outer space, I wiggled into the extremely tight cockpit of the car. The cockpit is so small, the steering wheel had to be removed to climb in and out of the car. A five-point harness/restraint system was then tightened, and wrist restraints were attached to my wrists and the lap belt buckle was fastened.

As tight as it was and even thought the wrist restraints intentionally prevented me from raising my hands above the steering wheel as a safety measure, everything was within reach—shift and "kill" buttons on the left side of the wheel, fire bottle buttons on the right side of the wheel, and two chute levers on the right side of the cockpit. The sparse instrument panel had only a tachometer and oil and fuel pressure gauges—no speedometer. For determining approximate speeds we would use what we called a whiz wheel, which took into account wheel diameter, rpms, and rear end gear ratio.

As we approached the starting line, the safety inspector gave the car a final visual inspection. He noticed that a set screw on the right forward axle had backed out. Leonard quickly tightened the screw. No obvious leaks, seat belts were tightened, and we got a thumbs up. Leonard jumped into the push truck, and we were off.

I remember it like it was yesterday. Leonard was in the push truck behind me, I heard the horn honk, let the clutch out, eased on the gas pedal. What a sensation! We finally hit the right numbers to make it run. I saw 6,500–7,000 rpms on the tachometer as I pushed the button selecting second gear. My other two successful runs in the car weren't particularly fast, maybe 180 or 190, but when you sit in a car with your butt six inches off the ground going that fast, it's a rush. Safety is paramount, and because of the high speeds, the car was equipped with two parachutes to assist in stopping it. As I shifted into second gear, the RPMs dropped off slightly, but they soon climbed back to the 6,500-7,000 RPM range. I shifted into third, or high, gear and the car continued to accelerate. I remember seeing the tachometer climb back up, but I have no recollection beyond that point.

That day, the salt was very rough, making for unfavorable conditions, which is what I was to prove. No one knows at what speed the car crashed, but from my final tachometer readings, it could have been in excess of 250 miles per hour. What happened, we'll never know. I can only imagine the car rolled many times. The wrist restraints, which are supposed to keep the driver's hands and arms in the cockpit, didn't work as they had been designed. Centrifugal force threw my arms out of the cockpit, allowing the roll cage to shear off my left hand and damage my other hand to the extent that it had to be amputated.

Hand amputations from high-speed rollovers such as mine are not new at Bonneville. I know of at least two other racers who lost hands in similar accidents. It seems that wrist restraints don't work as advertised.

Chapter 10

Atrophy and Other Obstacles

The ensuing 10 days of my life are lost forever in my blurred memory. I remember dreaming that I was in the First Aid tent at the salt flats, trying to tell someone the course is rough, but no one would listen. I was then told I'd be transferred to a hospital. But why? Still no one would answer me when I described the rough course. I heard lots of voices and I tried to talk to them, but I got no reply. I thought, "They are talking about me! It's a one-way conversation." I finally realized the car had crashed, and I had suffered some traumatic injuries, but I didn't know what they were. This medically induced slumber was frustrating because no one would answer my questions. I was aware when they transferred me from the intensive-care unit to a hospital room. It seemed as if I immediately woke up. I saw Mary Ann, my daughter, Shelley, who lives in Arizona with her husband and three kids, and our neighbor Sheila. Mary Ann smiled at me and said, "Honey, the car crashed. Your hands are gone." I knew I crashed the car and I had suffered a traumatic injury so I wasn't surprised to hear "your hands are gone." My initial thoughts were, "When can I get outta' here? When can I get on with life? When can I start flying again?" I knew I would fly again. I would just have to figure out how.

Obstacles. My whole life, it seemed, had involved surmounting obstacles. I would just brush them away and keep on marching. But this was a BIG obstacle—one that would plague me for the rest of my life. Part of me was saying, "I can do this! It will not stop me from doing all of the things I love and have done in the past." But another part of me was scared to death.

The people at the University of Utah Medical Center were efficient and performed their work well. After spending two weeks there, Mary Ann and I took a commercial flight to Sacramento, where I was to continue to recuperate and receive physical therapy at the University of California, Davis, Medical Center in Sacramento, which was closer to home. But in contrast to the protected environment of the Utah medical center, I felt like I was in the criminal ward of the hospital, and it seemed like a nightmare.

In Sacramento, I was assigned a room with another patient who had been shot and was rapping to the hip-hop music he was listening to. There was an apparent drug dealer nearby, who had been shot by a policeman, and another guy in the ward had a broken neck because he crashed a stolen car. There was only one guy who appeared normal. He had been injured in a bicycle accident. I think we were the only two people on that floor with insurance, and we were paying everyone else's way. My friend Marti Childs knew the hospital director and called him to complain. The next day I was moved to a room with more acceptable roommates.

One of my first sessions with a therapist was one of the worst days of my life when she told me I would probably never drive a car again. I asked her, "How do you expect me to get to the airport?" She replied, "Why do you want to go to the airport?" That session ended abruptly, and I never saw her again.

About two weeks after being admitted to the hospital in Sacramento, I was fitted with a set of body-powered hooks. My friend Gary Childs had been searching the Internet for different prosthetic options and discovered the higher-tech devices known as myoelectric hands are capable of far more refined motion and control. However, the physician assigned to me was unconvinced. I told him that the myoelectric hands were the only type of hands that would allow me to do what I wanted to do—fly airplanes. I needed a prescription for them, but he would prescribe only the hooks.

After being released from the hospital in Sacramento and arriving home in Vacaville, I had severe insomnia. That's also when I realized just what I *couldn't* do. Mary Ann had to do everything for me, and it was so frustrating for me, and I know it was taking a toll on her. Mary Ann said I went through an angry period about the time I got the hooks. I *was* angry! Mostly because no one would listen to me. I knew I would fly again, but the doctors and many other people thought I was delusional from the head injury.

During a follow-up appointment, the doctor brought in the hooks and I had a crushing feeling thinking about myself wearing hooks on both arms.

They were so freakish looking, and I knew they wouldn't work for me. One of the problems with the hooks is that they require you to wear a harness on your back. That's okay if you're missing only one hand, but I had to wear a double harness—and putting them on was almost impossible to do by myself. I hated them, and I went into a deep depression. I thought about ways I could commit suicide without harming anyone else. Possibly jumping off a bridge. A doctor prescribed a medication for depression and anxiety, but it made me feel like a zombie, which I hated worse.

The desire to fly was what kept me on track and overpowered the thoughts of suicide, and myoelectric hands were the only prostheses that would allow me to attain my goal. Because body-powered prosthetics cost a fraction of what myoelectric hands cost, the insurance companies tended to push the lower-cost hook prosthetics. I finally persuaded my primary care physician in Sacramento to give me a prescription for myoelectric hands. Then I went on a search to find a myoelectric prosthesis suited for me. I initially selected a company that I came to call Brand X in San Diego.

Brand X was like a craft class in high school. They used basic plaster of Paris molds like all other prosthetists use to build the socket out of fiberglass and carbon fiber.

They finished my hands, brought them to me late in the day, and said, "Here are your hands, and here are the batteries, but they aren't charged. Take them home and put them in the charger, then try them out." Because of their unprofessional service, I call them Brand X.

When you first get the hands they need a lot of maintenance, so being 600 miles from the company in San Diego, I couldn't run down there every week to have them adjusted or get additional training. The owner of the company was a heavy cigarette smoker and just reeked with smoke. He was never on time (punctuality was not his game), they'd put me in a tiny room, take the hands and leave me there for hours while they worked on them. It was a factory, and they had about six of these rooms. So I was sitting in this cubicle one day waiting for my hands, and I noticed an amputee golfer magazine. On the back cover was an advertisement for ProControl prosthetic hands, and it said, "The most advanced hands available." They were made by Harold Sears, a genuine gentleman, in Salt Lake City. When I got home, I called Harold Sears and asked him, "Where can I see your hands?" He told me to contact one of his dealers, NovaCare in San Francisco. So I made an appointment and went to NovaCare. There I met a prosthetist named Wallis Faraday, who was from New Zealand. He fitted me with a pair of hands, and helped me work with my insurance company to get another set of hands.

Both companies used the same Ottobock prosthetic hands made in Germany, but NovaCare provided much better service than Brand X. I believe location, professionalism, billing procedures, availability and honesty are what make a prosthetic company successful. The hands are basically all the same.

About the same time I was introduced to NovaCare, a television producer from the East Coast contacted me through NovaCare because he was working on TV documentary program called *Body Human 2000*. It was an hour-long show to be broadcast on primetime CBS, and I was one of three people featured in the program. The CBS crew filmed me every weekend for a month, beginning with trying to reconstruct the accident. They talked about what happened to me, how the hands are made, how they work, what I can do today with the hands—specifically fly airplanes. Although it was filmed in the mid-1990s, it is still shown occasionally on science/learning TV channels. NovaCare saw me as a marketing tool, so they asked if I'd travel to Pennsylvania for a disability expo. I agreed and spent the day at their booth, showing my video, demonstrating my hands and answering many questions.

133

These myoelectric hands work exactly like your hands do. For instance, when you want to open and close your hand, your brain tells your hand to open or close by flexing a muscle. Anytime you flex a muscle, it emits a minute electrical signal. The sensors in my prosthetic arm touch the muscle reading an electrical impulse that sends a message to a receiver which transmits it to an electrical motor that opens, closes or rotates the hands, depending how the muscle is flexed. To do that, the socket of the prosthetic into which I insert my limbs must precisely fit the contours of my limbs. Proper functioning requires exact alignment of the sensors as well as proper pressure against my limbs.

Limbs commonly shrink as a result of muscle atrophy after an injury. Atrophy or significant weight loss requires the prosthesis to be re-sized in order to restore contact between the muscle and the sensor. The effects of muscle atrophy can take up to about a year to stabilize following an injury. Because of that, amputees are advised to wait about a year after their injury before being fitted with myoelectrics. But I was fitted right away. As a result, my prostheses had to be rebuilt a couple of times. I learned that one way to reduce atrophy is to wear a tight wrap around the limb to compress it and speed up the atrophy process.

Chapter 11

Adaptation

When I got the new hands, I had to devise new ways to do literally everything. Simple things that everyone else takes for granted—opening a door with a rotating knob, brushing my teeth, answering the phone, even signing my name—became monumental challenges. I tackled them one by one.

One of the first things I learned with my new hands was how to use them to feed myself. Mary Ann wrapped inch-thick foam around a fork so I could better grasp it in my hand, and I quickly learned that I have to look at the hand while I'm picking up an object. At nighttime I'm not that good with the hands because visual acuity is very important.

I never wear long sleeves because the hands are just too bulky to put them through a shirt or coat sleeve. The wrist does rotate but there is no back and forth movement, and I have to see my hand to make sure it is closed in order to slip on the sleeve of a shirt or jacket. How do I reach in my pocket and get a pen? It's very difficult without dropping it. Tying a pen to a string around my neck might help, but even to position a pen in my hand to write is difficult. It takes a lot of work, and if I drop it, that's frustrating. The rigidity of my prosthetic fingers won't allow me to pick it up.

I am capable of flying a Boeing 737 or McDonnell Douglas DC-9, but the minor collateral duties, such as putting on a necktie or taking off my coat in the cockpit are very difficult. Trying to pick up the metal logbook that's 12 by 18 inches, then thumbing through it to find the page we're on today, is a challenge. Thumbing through the previous pages to see the history of the airplane and then signing it as an acceptance of the airplane is difficult. Just thumbing through a magazine is a monumental sequence of tasks for me. If you tell me to "Go to page 18," I have a hard time. As sophisticated as the myoelectric hands are, they can mimic only some of the functions of human hands. While the prosthetics can grasp large objects, the refined movements to pick up or manipulate small objects are nearly impossible, so I've had to make adaptations.

Suppose I want to grab a hot dog for lunch. I never use a wallet. I keep my ID card and money in my shirt pocket, because that's the only pocket I can see into to grab what I'm trying to reach for. Now to get $2.98 out of that pocket is tough—I can't pick up coins. I can take bills out and hand them to a cashier and get change back, try to dump coins into my pocket without dropping them, then fold the bills so that I can get them in the pocket.

I can't carry a tray of food at fast-food restaurants, and I have difficulty unwrapping food items. In the beginning, Mary Ann was always getting me these big, juicy hamburgers and I had to say, "Please get me a basic hamburger with bun and cheese," because the cheese sticks to the meat and bun and it's easier to eat. I don't want anything that's drippy, because I'll wear it.

Paper cups are a disaster because the lack of sense of feeling causes me to crush them. A myoelectric hand called the SUVA hand was developed to counteract that. It has a sensor to detect slippage and automatically tightens as an object slips from your grasp. Hanger Prosthetics gave me a pair to try out. I found that it didn't work very well for me because the hands were always moving, and I couldn't get them to work the way they were supposed to. I have settled on always using straws to drink, but I regularly test new products for Hanger.

The frustrations have never ended. When I drop a piece of paper on the floor at home, I have to get down on all fours to pick it up because I never wear my hands in the house. I drink water out of the faucet as kids do—it's easier than getting a cup.

I manage showering well. I have a liquid soap dispenser on the wall. However, going to the bathroom and other aspects of personal hygiene are real problems. For toilet functions, a bidet is a necessity. I use an electric shaver. I can't use shaving cream or a blade anymore—I might cut my lips off.

I know of two bilateral amputee pilots. One of them lives in Vacaville, and he flies airplanes with two hooks. He was the most helpful guy I met. He showed me how he flew airplanes. He had lost his hands as an electrician in Hawaii and had about 20 more years of experience than I did. He was very motivating for me because he showed me that things can be done. He could button shirts, flies and zip zippers with special hooks. I watched him and thought, "There's got to be an easier way to do this." So I found an easier way—I don't have any buttons on my clothing; I wear only pullover shirts. All of my pants have an elastic waistband, no buttons, and no fly in the front. I can't use a belt, either. I seldom wear socks, and all of my shoes are slip-ons.

I rarely wear shirts with collars because the collars flip inside, and I can't pull them out. I keep my collared shirts on hangers in my closet all facing the same way. I have to bite the collar and the shirt and carefully put it on and hope the collar doesn't flip over to the inside. If it does, I take the shirt off and start over again. I mainly wear T-shirts with pockets.

Every day is a challenge, but every day I get better at figuring out how to do things. I make my own coffee. I buy coffee bags, and I have a paper cutter in my office to get the bag open. Then I grab it with my teeth until the coffee bag falls out. I put the cup under the water and then put it in the microwave. After it's hot, I put a washcloth over the hot cup to pick it up with my stumps and carry it to the table. Then I get a straw to drink it. Every time I go visit friends, they have straws for me, which is nice, but they always take a flex straw and bend it over for me. It's frustrating because it drips.

Handwriting is very difficult. I can write out of necessity. Picking up a pen or pencil is difficult with the myoelectric hands, and even when I'm holding it, I have a tough time using it. Imagine if you had a pencil that's two feet long, but you could hold onto only the eraser. Could you control it? That's the problem I have, because where my arm stops, the prosthetic extends another foot or so and the pencil is beyond that. I can write, but not very well. My letters are big. I use the computer for my checkbook entries and all of my writing.

Every day I pick up a new skill, but it all takes a lot of patience. If I want to write a check to pay a bill, I can type all of the information for the check on my computer, print it out and tear it off. Then I have to get my pen, position it properly in my hand and turn off the hand so I don't drop the pen. I hold the check with my left stump and sign the check with my right prosthetic hand. Next, I get a window envelope to put the check inside, but the envelope has no extra space so it's difficult to push the check in. After I manage to get the check inside the envelope, I need to turn it over to make sure the address shows through the window. With that accomplished, I seal the envelope and pick up my roll of stamps. Next I've got to peel the little stamp off the little paper it's stuck to and try to put the stamp on the letter in the right spot, hoping it doesn't get stuck on the desk on the way to the letter. I've got stamps stuck to my desk here and there that never made it to the envelope. Functions that someone with two hands can do in seconds can take me much, much longer.

To change a print cartridge in my printer, I have to get my letter opener and hold it just right, again locking my hand so the letter opener doesn't fall out. I push down on the cartridge to release it. I then stick the letter opener under the old cartridge to try to pop it out. I know I can't open the box with the new cartridge, so I may tear off 50 little pieces with my teeth trying to get the box open. After I get the box open, I see the cartridge in a plastic container with tape around it. I take my paper cutter and cut it open, then I manage to place the new cartridge in the printer using the letter opener.

Nothing is easy. Zip lock bags are terrible. If I never see another zip lock bag, I'll be happy.

Rotary door knobs are difficult for me. First I have to see the knob to grab it, close my hand around it then

141

move my whole body to rotate the knob. At home we have levers instead of door knobs.

A friend of mine, Sheri Marshall, is a one-armed pilot who works for Federal Express as a ground instructor. She wrote a good book called *One Can Do It*. She lost her arm in a washing machine mishap at a young age. Her book tells how she overcame her physical impairment to become an airline transport-rated pilot, inventor, potter, scuba diver, drag boat racer, author and mother of two daughters. She talks about how she changes her kid's diapers and how she hangs wallpaper with one arm.

The best thing for a newly disabled person is to find another person with the same disability. Unilateral amputees are not as helpful to me in trying to figure out how to do things, because they have use of their other hand. Bilateral amputees constitute a very small percentage of all amputees. Upper-extremity amputees total only about 10 percent of all amputees, and we have trouble finding a source for practical assistance. Maybe we tend to be a little more creative because of that. Everything is difficult—everything is a challenge.

I think the biggest challenge I had was for other people to accept the fact that disabled people can do things. For example, getting my driver's license back.

I had to take a driving test to get my license back. The California Department of Motor Vehicles restricted my driver's license, and essentially I was a student driver all over again—I could drive only with a licensed driver in the car with me. I had a pickup truck with an automatic transmission and a 1987 Corvette with a manual transmission at the time. I decided to drive the Corvette for the driving test just to make an impression. I practiced driving it at the Nut Tree Airport with the intention of surprising the examiner with my ability. After I took the driving test, the instructor said, "Good job!" I said, "I know. You think I came to fail?" As far as I'm concerned, I practiced for that. I don't go to fail. If I'm not prepared, I don't go. He's probably still telling the story about the driving student taking his test with no hands, driving a stick shift Corvette.

After passing the test, I could drive the Corvette okay, but it would stall on me all the time, and the hardest thing was turning the ignition switch. Rotary things are a problem for me. Toggle switches and levers are easy, but a rotary switch is a challenge. I sold my truck and Corvette and bought a Lexus with an automatic transmission.

My car has two little plastic envelopes on the console—one with my driver's license, and one with a credit card, picture ID and grocery cards. I have trouble locking my car, because trying to carry a key is difficult. All of my keys have tie wraps on them and I put them in my shirt pocket so they stick out. But the challenge for me is how to push the button on the key to lock or unlock the door, or how to hold onto the key and put it in the door. I have to put the key in the lock and turn it with my other hand. Then I have to take the key out of the door, grab the tie wrap and hope I don't drop it, then put it in the ignition.

I'm the first person ever to be certified to fly airplanes with two myoelectric prostheses. I had about 20,000 hours of flight time before the accident. Under the same circumstances, a 100-hour pilot probably would not have gotten his medical clearance to fly. I also was very driven, and I fought to get my medical clearance back. It was not a fast process.

In March of 1994, only six months after my accident, I requested issuance of a third-class FAA certificate to reinstate my private pilot's license. I first went to Leroy

Brown, M.D., A.M.E. (aviation medical examiner), a flight surgeon in Sacramento. He gave me a flight physical and sent it to the FAA for approval. The request was denied because of concerns about my cognitive abilities after the accident. About the same time, American Airlines put me on temporary medical disability. In May of 1994, I requested reconsideration of my case by the FAA, but they again denied certification. I asked, "Why?" I was going through fits of frustration trying to figure out what I could do next to fight the bureaucracy.

I was determined to fly again, so that fall I obtained a commercial glider pilot's license for which a medical examination was not required. That's actually an "add-on" certificate to a pilot's license. The FAA requirements for individuals who have logged at least 40 hours of flight time as a pilot was at least three hours of flight time in a glider. That included 10 training flights with an instructor, 10 solo flights and three training flights in preparation for the practical test. I passed with flying colors and had hoped that would impress upon the FAA that I could still fly airplanes and it would help them make the decision to reinstate my medical. It might have shown my determination, but it didn't convince them.

My friend Mike Deaner, who lives in Santa Maria, said, "We've got a doctor here who is really good at solving these problems. His name is Dr. Henry Rowe." So I flew down to Santa Maria with my friend Gary Childs, who is also a pilot. We met with Dr. Rowe, an M.D. and Aviation Medical Examiner (A.M.E.), and he gave me lots of encouragement but said it would take some work. Dr. Rowe, who graduated with a degree in mechanical engineering from MIT before attending medical school, had worked for the FAA and said the most powerful tool he had was that he knew all of the secretaries on a first-name basis. He said when you send something to the FAA it goes on the stack and it stays on that stack sometimes for a very long time. So Dr. Rowe could call Mabel and say, "Mabel, pull that piece of paper out of the stack." So we worked, and worked, and worked.

Finally the FAA sent a letter that instructed me to 1) undergo a comprehensive follow-up neurological evaluation to assess the current status of my cognitive functioning; 2) complete an evaluation of my prostheses in the altitude chamber at the FAA Civil Aeromedical Institute (CAMI) in Oklahoma City; 3) take a third-class medical flight test; and 4) undergo a follow-up cardiovascular evaluation because of my previously documented hypertension, which was controlled with medication. I couldn't understand why I needed to be tested in a pressure chamber that simulated the atmosphere at 40,000 feet—in the airline, the cockpit is pressurized to the equivalent of about 8,000 feet. I would fly 40,000 feet with a third class medical. But the FAA wanted me to jump through these hoops.

While I was in Oklahoma City, I visited the Scott Sabolich Prosthetics and Research Center. Some of the Sabolich Center's personnel accompanied me to the pressure chamber. They never told me why they were doing this test, but I think their biggest concern was that these hands may explode and do damage to other people. So I sat in the pressure chamber with an oxygen mask on, and they took me up to a simulation of about 40,000 feet. They wanted to see me open and close the hand at 40,000 feet. They then did an explosive decompression down to 18,000 feet, and I had to open and close my hand again. After that, they took me down to sea level and we were finished. To this day, I don't really know what they were trying to accomplish.

Before I became involved with Dr. Rowe, I had applied to the FAA several times, and I always got letters back from Washington, D.C., that said, "No." No reason given, not even a spark of hope. They just flat said, "No." Well, I can't take "No" for an answer! If they would have said, "No, not at this time, but as you make progress..." I could have accepted something like that, but they just said, "No."

In April of 1995, the FAA authorized me to take a demonstratability check ride. So I called the FAA person in Sacramento and requested a check ride. I flew a Cessna 182, because I wanted to fly a relatively complex high-performance airplane. I didn't want them to put limitations on my medical clearance as a result of flying a low-powered airplane during the check ride. I flew to Sacramento Executive Airport with Kerry Roberson and met with the examiner. He said, "We'll take off and fly around and see how you do." So I got into the airplane and put on my seatbelt, which is one of the hardest things I can do. I called ground control, taxied out, called the tower and got permission to take off. We took off and he said, "Turn downwind." I said, "Okay. Do you want to shoot some landings?" He said, "No. We're done." So we turned downwind, and of course I flew very well, and landed, and he said, "Good job!"

Flight medicals are designated first, second and third class. The only person required to have a first-class certification is an airline captain. Second class certification is required for someone who flies for hire, and third class is for private pilots.

The examiner gave me a third-class medical, which prevented me from flying for the airlines. Even though a third-class medical awards private-pilot privileges only, essentially he re-validated all of my ratings at the private-pilot level.

I asked him if he could renew my CFI (certified flight instructor) rating. I'd had my CFI since 1965 without a break. According the FAA, you have to renew a CFI rating every two years in a clinic or through practical use, and mine had expired when I was in the hospital, and I couldn't attend a clinic. He asked his fellow FAA evaluator and said, "Sure can." So all of my CFI ratings were reinstated.

I've since tried to get a second-class medical rating, but the FAA thus far has refused to issue that.

Chapter 12

Spins, Loops and Rolls

After winning the battle with the FAA to get my medical certification reinstated, I was ready to show the rest of the world what an able-bodied, double amputee could really do. Confident that I would fly airplanes again, I had insisted on installation of a turn-off switch in both prosthetic hands to lock them closed so I could keep a grip on an airplane stick. The hands are muscle-activated, so if I were to relax, a hand could possibly open up and I wouldn't know it unless I actually looked down at it. As extraordinary as these hands are, my version cannot detect or transmit feeling, so visual acuity is essential.

My medical authorization was issued too late for the 1995 aerobatics season, so I spent the winter looking for a new aerobatic airplane and getting reacquainted with the world of aerobatic flying. It was obvious that the confined cockpit of my beloved hand-built Pitts S1S would no longer be suitable for me to fly aerobatics competitions. The cockpit was difficult for me to get in and out of, and because of the bulkier myoelectric hands, the confined cockpit just wasn't satisfactory. So I began my search for an airplane that would work for me.

Several years earlier, during my first trip to South Africa in 1992, I got my first introduction of the Zlin 50, a Czechoslovakian-made monoplane, a three-time world champion and one of the first to unseat the famous

Mike in his Zlin 50

Pitts Special S1S. Watching it fly in an air show left a lasting impression. It was a sleek, low-maintenance, all-metal airplane with a huge cockpit, a multi-adjustable seat and everything within easy reach. The Zlin 50 was manufactured by Moravan Aircraft in the 1970s.

I was lucky to find a Zlin 50 for sale in Northern California, just south of Modesto, and the seller delivered the airplane to my hangar at Vacaville's Nut Tree Airport in the spring of 1996. Since it was a new airplane for me, I was cautious, but I flew it the same day it was delivered. By my second flight, I had explored most of the aerobatic maneuvers in the Aresti (official record of maneuvers) catalog with success. With its performance and comfort, the Zlin was just what I had been looking for.

Before my accident, I was very much involved in the five regional aerobatics contests in California. They were held in Paso Robles, Delano, Willows, Taft and Borrego Springs. The Delano contest had special significance for Mary Ann and me in 1996. There, with aerobatic pilot and preacher Roger Rourke presiding, Mary Ann and I were married.

I had been competing in the "advanced" category and practicing for the "unlimited" category in my Pitts. I knew that after my accident I needed to take it a step at

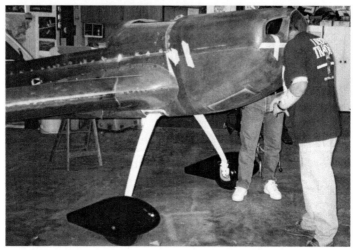

Akrotech G202 construction

a time, so I flew three sportsman (or beginning) category contests in 1996. I captured one first-place and two second-place finishes—so the most precious trophy for me was the self-satisfaction of my successful return to competition aerobatics. The following year, I competed in the "intermediate" category before moving on to other things.

In 1997 I was combining contests with air shows, which was difficult, because aerobatics contests are flown at a much higher altitude, and precision is essential. In contrast, air show pilots are required to fly at a lower altitude to excite the crowd, and precision isn't as crucial because they're not being judged. At the time, I was the only pilot in the world with two myoelectric hands to hold a zero-altitude aerobatics waiver—meaning that no altitude restrictions were placed on me. Word traveled fast that a bilateral amputee was flying air shows, and I drew plenty of news media attention.

After traveling almost every weekend to air shows and contests, and asking Mary Ann to drive the car, I realized that we needed an aerobatic airplane with two seats. I had seen an Akrotech 200, a single-seat monoplane, at an air show and discovered through the Akrotech website that a two-seat version called the 202 was available in kit form.

Mary Ann and I traveled up to Scappoose, Oregon, and spent a pleasant night at the Barnstormer Inn at Scappoose Airport. The next day we toured the nearby Akrotech facilities. I was impressed, and after quick calculations, I said to Mary Ann, "With this fuel capacity we can fly nonstop from Calexico to Cabo San Lucas." She replied with a "go-ahead" smile. When I added, "upside down," her smile quickly turned to a frown.

Roger Rourke, who had married us at the 1996 Delano contest, had agreed to start building the 202. Roger is quite a character, he's a machinist, race car builder/driver, an Oshkosh grand champion builder and sometimes preacher. But when he became too busy with other projects to finish my 202, my good friend

Mike discussing the Akrotech with his good friend Barry Wells

Sean deRosier volunteered to retrieve it from Roger's home and return it to my hangar at Nut Tree Airport. Sean also agreed to complete construction of the aircraft. I was pleased because I couldn't think of anyone more motivated or more qualified than this young man.

I had known Sean since he was a kid. He was just like any other high school student, except he hung out at the airport about 20 hours a day. His first project, beginning with a radio- controlled (R/C) model aircraft, led to his restoration of a Cessna 150 and his qualification for a private pilot's certificate before high school graduation. He went on to college and eventually earned his A&P mechanic's rating. Sean completed the construction phase of my Akrotech in about two years.

With his father, Ben, Sean went on to build his own aerobatic aircraft he called Cabo Wabo "SkyRocker," and performed as an aerobatic pilot at air shows across the country. In 1999, I flew with Gerrit Brandt in my 202, and Sean in his SkyRocker to the Experimental Aircraft Association's (EAA) annual convention in Oshkosh, Wisconsin. Sean's airplane won an Outstanding Workmanship Award and mine won a "Lindy" Championship. For one builder to have two aircraft winning trophies the same year at Oshkosh is an outstanding feat. Sean was like a son to me. I had so much faith in him. I helped him financially in his early business days, and he always paid back the loans.

In October 2004, Sean was one of the first pilots to perform aerobatics during the air show at Marine Corps Air Station Miramar near San Diego. While doing one of

Akrotech G202 in flight over Vacaville

his well-practiced aerobatic maneuvers, he failed to pull out of a steep dive and crashed between the two runways. He suffered severe internal injuries in the accident and died en route to the hospital. He was only 31 years old, a gifted young man. I'm glad I was able to spend some time with him, and I miss him very much.

When I lived near Auburn, I met a talented artist named Jim Moser. Jim did outstanding hand-pinstriping and painted graphics on anything with a motor—race cars, motorcycles, airplanes and trucks. His work was exquisite, and I had already decided he would be the one to paint my 202. Jim, with his equally talented business partner Sheila Bovin, began the paint process with some sketches of different paint schemes based on color choices and the need for lines that accentuate the different axes of the aircraft for aerobatics competition. To help visualize the paint scheme, another friend of mine, Kerry Roberson—a mechanic, pilot, radio-controlled aircraft builder, and retired Air Force major—built a quarter-scale model of my Akrotech. Jim painted the graphics scheme on the model to visually see the paint scheme, and he duplicated it on the 202.

FAA Designated Airworthiness Representative (DAR) Dave Morss agreed to do the initial inspection and issue the special airworthiness certificate. Dave was a Formula One racer at the Reno Air Races, and I had met him several years before. He flew in from Palo Alto and verified that all the required paperwork, including aircraft registration, construction log, weight and balance, was in order. The airplane had been properly prepared for his inspection, and easily passed the 45-minute procedure.

Since Dave had performed many flights of experimental aircraft, including an Akrotech 202, he agreed to do the initial test flight. I added him to my insurance policy, and Dave was soon in the air. He encountered no major problems, and later that afternoon I took the 202 up for some loops and rolls. It performed as I had hoped it would. Due to the long completion time, other interests had begun to compete with my flying time. I was by then taking commercial flights all over the country to give presentations for my prosthetic company, NovaCare, demonstrating the capabilities of the equipment for doctors, therapists, and prosthetists as well as consulting other amputees. Because I was a bilateral amputee and I flew airplanes, NovaCare liked to use me as a "show and tell" display.

I traveled to South Africa for the first time in 1992 (prior to the accident) to attend the South African

Experimental Aircraft Association (EAA) Convention in Margate with my Vacaville neighbor Jeff Sharman, and to deliver an airplane that he had sold during the convention. Owner of Jarlin Aviation, Jeff had shipped a 7KCAB Citabria to South Africa and located a buyer in an area of South Africa called the Wilderness. During the southbound delivery trip along the coast of the Indian Ocean, we flew over the surfing mecca of Cape St. Francis, had an overnight stay in Port Alfred—where the runway consisted of one square mile of grass—and finally delivered the aircraft in the town of George.

During our stay, I met Scully Levin, a 747 captain with South African Airways, and a former South African aerobatics champion. In 1995 I invited Scully to come to the United States to fly my Pitts S1S at the Reno Air Races, and he won the Silver Biplane race that September.

An enduring friendship began, and in 1998 Scully asked me if I would be interested in flying the aerobatic air show circuit in South Africa, which ended with Aerospace Africa. That's the largest air show in the Southern Hemisphere, attended by more than 500,000 people from throughout the world. Every aircraft-related business in the world was represented in acres of hangars located at the Waterkloof South African Air Force Base near the capital town of Pretoria.

I agreed to fly, and Scully introduced me to Mike van Ginkel, director general of the Aero Club of South Africa, who made all of the arrangements for my trip. South African Airways provided four first-class round-trip airline tickets, Budget rent-a-car supplied us with a VW Kombi van, MTN provided cellular phones, and the Aero Club paid for lodging. Hooch Beverages, along with aircraft owners Brad Bennett and Andrew Christou, provided a Zlin 50 aircraft for my aerobatic shows.

Mary Ann and I were joined on this trip by our California neighbors Jeff Sharman, who operated an aircraft repair and retrieval business while in South Africa, and his wife, Sheila, who was a professional

Mike in the Hooch Zlin 50, ready to fly aerobatics in the five-day South African airshow Africa Aerospace

skydiver in South Africa. Sheila grew up in Kenya and Jeff in Johannesburg.

The altitude at Waterkloof AFB is about 5,000 feet and the temperature was around 80 degrees during my practices. That combination decreases aircraft performance, which the pilot must be aware of. I'll never forget one practice day. Scully called and said, "I've got to practice with the South African Airways formation flight team in the 'Harvard,' and you can fly backseat." The British named this advanced trainer aircraft the "Harvard." The U.S. Air Force recognized the aircraft as an AT-6, and the U.S. Navy version was called the SNJ.

We met Scully at his home and headed to the South African Airways headquarters, where Scully gave us a quick tour of their full-motion simulators, including the South African Classic aircraft division. As we entered the huge Classic Division hangar, my jaw dropped. There in front of me were three perfectly restored Harvards, plus three more under restoration, two DC-4s, two DC-3s, a Lodestar, an early jet and a Junkers JU52 tri-motor. All would be award winners if entered in the world-famous Experimental Aircraft Association's Oshkosh Air Show. The DC-3s, 4s and JU-52 are still used in the South African Airways Charter Division.

After two days of practice, we loaded up our VW Kombi and headed to the EAA Convention in Margate. After a night in the beautiful Drakensberg Mountains and a quick trip around Durban, we arrived in the coastal town of Margate. I was disappointed that poor weather there prevented me from flying in the air show, but I was able to admire 100 or more homebuilt aircraft that were there on display, and I was honored by being asked to assist in the award presentation at the closing ceremony and dinner.

Upon returning to Johannesburg, I figured on spending a leisurely week ending with an air show. How wrong I was! Jeff Sharman had my days quickly filled with TV and radio appearances, newspaper interviews, school visits and the highlight of the trip—a visit to the Hope School.

The Hope School is a convalescent school for disabled children. Although it was a holiday week, about 100 children filed into the auditorium to greet me. I was almost in shock. I observed kids with birth defects, amputations, muscular dystrophy, polio and other debilitating conditions. Soon, however, all I saw were smiles. Every child was so polite and smiled. One little girl had no arms, only hands attached to her shoulders. She smiled as she said, "Shake my hand, please." I was so amazed by her during my presentation, and not until

I finished did I notice that the girl sitting next to her had no legs. I also met a young man named Tommy, who was about 13 years old, with advanced muscular dystrophy. Later that morning, as Jeff and I left the school, we noticed the kids all waving from the curb. Not one disability was obvious—only kids with smiling faces.

The air show days became fast and furious: two shows daily, punctuated by Scully leading the Shurlok Pitts team and the South African Airways Harvard Team. Other performers included Peter Celliers in an Extra 300, Glen Dell in a Pitts S2S, the Smirnoff Pitts

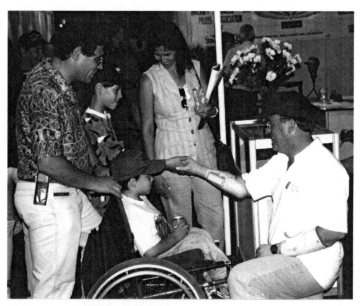

Mike meeting Tommy from Hope School

Team, the Crunchie Stearman with a wingwalker, South African Airways DC-4 fly-bys, tailslides in an antique French Mirage jet fighter, and numerous other fly-bys by aircraft manufacturers. Between shows, I was most often in the Aero Club booth greeting dozens of visitors, who all wanted to see the "Yank with the funny hands" and how they work. It seemed like I shook hands with about 1,000 people a day.

After my last flight, I was summoned to the announcer's stand. As I neared the stand I noticed Tommy from Hope School in his specially equipped wheelchair with his mother at his side. When I acknowledged him by name, he was grinning ear to ear. I asked his mother to push his wheelchair to my airplane for pictures. When he arrived, I asked if he would like to sit in the airplane cockpit for pictures. With his mom's help, we lifted him into the cockpit. Tommy's smile was so big, you could hardly see the airplane.

As Africa Aerospace ended, the sightseeing portion of our trip began. We spent the first night in the fantastic Sun City. Who could imagine finding in the middle of the high South African plains one of the finest resorts in the world? Gambling casinos, golf courses, and game preserves were all part of the landscape. You could surf in the huge wave pool (imagine seeing elephants from the crest of a wave) or jog on the golf course, which had signs that said, "Do not retrieve golf balls from the water hazards. Crocodiles have been sighted."

At Kruger Park, we saw lions, zebras, giraffes, Cape buffalo, elephants and baboons, and more. We spent four nights in Lindsay Castle, a replica of a 1500 AD castle near the town of Knysna. The closest parking was a half-mile away, and for the rest of the way we followed a footpath over the sand and rocks. If we arrived after sunset, Joe, the caretaker, would lead us in by the sound of him playing bagpipes. Nestled just above the surf in a dense jungle environment, the castle had minimal electricity, a great fireplace, a good supply of candles and sufficient water.

The entire month in South Africa was a trip of a lifetime that I will never forget. For it was there that I realized my next mission—to work with children.

I will always fondly associate this 1998 South African visit with my friend Jeff Sharman, who died 15 years later, on February 13, 2013. The 1959 vintage Avions Fairey Tipsey Nipper T-66 aerobatic plane he was flying crashed near Winters, California, after a wing broke loose. Jeff was 68 years old.

Chapter 13

A Touch of Understanding

My experiences working with kids in South Africa had been extremely rewarding, and I thought this might be the inspiration I had been seeking to allow me to move forward with a new life's mission. I always had been terrified of public speaking in front of an audience of more than one person. But soon after I had recovered from the accident, I spoke to a group of head trauma patients, and I realized that talking about my accident was great therapy for me. I knew no one was going to challenge me about the subject matter, because it was something I knew intimately well.

Early retirement was a considerable predicament for me. Unable to continue my profession as an airline pilot, I suddenly found myself with a lot of extra time, and I was bored. One morning in 1997, as I sipped my cup of coffee while reading the *Sacramento Bee* newspaper, a story in the Metro section captured my interest. It was about a group of volunteers who toured schools in Northern California, giving presentations on disability awareness.

The program, called A Touch of Understanding, was founded by Leslie DeDora—whose phone number was included in the article. I called Leslie, told her about my accident and background, and asked if I could somehow fit into her program. I met with Leslie and her father, Ed, the following week to find out how the program operates. Leslie had been a volunteer and classroom aide at Green Hills elementary school in Granite Bay, California—about 15 miles northeast of Sacramento—when she observed kids with learning disabilities being teased by their peers. As a young child, Leslie couldn't quite understand why her developmentally disabled aunt looked like an adult but acted like a child. When Leslie's son Paul was 3 years old, she accompanied him to a children's museum where they observed a display on disabilities that included wooden crutches, an old wheelchair and a coffin. She says her son talked about it for months afterwards. Later, as a volunteer in her young son's classroom, Leslie observed how the "able-bodied" students at times tormented those who seemed slower than the rest since it was fairly new for children with disabilities to be "mainstreamed" into regular classrooms. At that point in 1992 she began planning her program to help children with disabilities be understood, appreciated and welcomed into the social circles, and to have a fun, "normal" childhood.

When I joined the program, it was staffed only by Leslie, Ed, and a couple of able-bodied volunteers. I was the first disabled person to join the program. Leslie would give a short presentation explaining about common disabilities, telling the kids we were all the same on the inside. She usually began her presentation with questions like, "Have you ever been 10 at because of something that wasn't at all funny to you?" She describes learning disabilities as "having all the right wires plugged into the wrong places." She says that just because some people use a wheelchair or have braces or prosthetic devices doesn't mean their hopes, dreams and intellect are different from yours or mine. After a short video presentation, Leslie would set up stations through which the kids would rotate. Each station was different; and the kids would get a chance to maneuver a wheelchair, learn the basics of using a walking cane, handle prosthetic devices, try to write looking through a mirror (which simulates dyslexia), write their name in Braille, and get an introduction to autism. The goal was to show the kids that we are all the same, but some of us just use different tools.

My first experience with A Touch of Understanding was simple; Leslie just tossed me into a classroom and said, "talk." The first time I talked, I didn't have anything prepared. I just told the kids about my hands. Now I include an introduction about Magy and service dogs, then I show the "Body Human 2000" video, which shows how I lost my hands, how the hands are made, how they work, and what I do for my favorite hobby. But I work up to it by asking, "What can I do with these hands? Can I drive a car?" You'd be surprised how many kids say, "no." Then I ask them, "So how did I get here from Vacaville? It's a long walk." Then I ask them, "Can I do pull ups?" The kids usually answer, "Yeh!" I say, "No, I can't. I can grab onto the bar, but as soon as I try to pull myself up, my hands will come off. Then I have to call my wife,

Mary Ann, and ask, 'Mary Ann, can you lend me a hand? Thank you!'" The kids all laugh. Then I ask them, "Can I do push ups?" One or two of the kids will usually say, "No." And I reply, "Sure, I can." Then I ask them, "Can I swim with these hands?" They answer, "oh, yeh—uh, no!" I always ask, "No? Why can't I?" Some kids will say, "because they're electronic." Then I say, "You're a good listener. You cannot get electronic circuitry wet. If I get them wet, they're going to spark and smoke, and my ears are going to light up." They laugh. I continue, "So I can't get my hands wet, but if I take them off, I can swim as well as you do." So if I want to go swimming, I take my hands off, lay them on the deck of the pool and jump in. But if I want to wash my car, I can't reach into a bucket of soapy water. I can walk in the rain, but I can't submerge these hands in water." I then ask them, "Do you think I could fly an airplane?" That usually gets mixed response, and I usually choose one child to ask, "If I could fly an airplane, could I fly it upside down? How do you tell if you're upside down?" I get all types of answers, but I say, "It's real simple. If your hair falls up, you're upside down. So if you're ever away on vacation with your parents, and you're in an airplane and your hair falls up, you're in trouble." Not only am I putting things into terms that kids can understand, but I'm getting them involved in the discussion by asking them questions.

After I go through my comedy routine, I tell them I'm going to show them a video that was made for TV several years ago. It was on prime-time TV, on CBS, and that it will show them how my hands were made, how they work and some of the things I can do with my hands.

After we watch the video I ask, "Did you like the video? You know why I can fly? Because I really wanted to do it. Just because I had a traumatic accident, does that mean I have to stop doing things? I've flown since I was in high school and there's no reason to stop. I may practice a little more, do things a little slower, but I can still do lots of things."

I ask, "From watching that video, can you tell what happened to me?" Some young man will say, "You crashed a race car." I'll say, "You're right, I crashed a race car on the - Salt Flats." Someone will ask, "Where are the Bonneville Salt Flats?" Surprisingly elementary school kids don't know. I tell them there's a lot of history there with the Donner Party, and Wendover Air Force Base, where crews were trained to drop the nuclear bombs that ended World War II. I say, "It's a huge area of salt as flat and as hard as your desktop. On the flats there's a long black line—about 20 miles long—that's the race course and you can go as fast as your car is capable of going. When I crashed the car, I don't know how fast I was going but the car was capable of speeds greater than 300 miles per hour. They tell me I never lost consciousness. They put me in a helicopter and flew me to the University of Utah Medical Center in Salt Lake City. When I got there the doctors gave me a shot that put me into a medically induced slumber. So I slept in the intensive-care unit ward for the next 10 days. But I wasn't really sleeping because I could hear the doctors talking about me. I realized that I had crashed the car and suffered a very severe injury. I didn't quite know what, but I knew it was really serious. So I woke up 10 days later, and my wife Mary Ann, my daughter, Shelley, and my neighbor Sheila were there. Mary Ann said to me, 'Honey, you crashed the car and your hands are gone.' I was not surprised when she told me my hands were gone, but I chose to start a new life using different tools."

Then I ask the kids, "How does someone run a marathon? It's real easy, it's so easy you'll never get it." I listen to the various answers from them, then I say, "All you do is take the first step, and the second step, and keep going and 26 miles and a couple of hundred yards later you're done. But if you won't start with that first step, you can't take the last step." Then I ask, "How do you do a big homework assignment? Does your teacher ever give you a homework assignment? Is that your teacher back there? She sure looks nice, but sometimes she's a meany, isn't she? So how do you do that big homework assignment? It's real easy. All you do is put the book in front of you and open that first page. You start with that first page. But if you don't start, you can't finish. Just like when I was in the hospital, I chose to start a new life—just like the marathon runner chooses to start a marathon, and the student chooses to start the homework assignment. You're very strong people, and you can choose to do whatever you want to do."

I always encourage the kids to stay in school. I say to them, "School is easy. You know how easy school is? When you get older and you start driving a car to high school or college you will get to the parking lot, look out at the campus and nothing is going to happen. But when you walk across the parking lot, into the building and sit down in class, something will happen. If you just attend class, you're probably going to do quite well."

As more incentive for kids to stay in school, I ask,

"How much do you think these hands cost?" I get every answer in the book—$1,000, $10,000—and there's always some wiseass kids who says, "They're free." I want to hear that, because I say, "No. Nothing is ever free." I say, "These hands cost about $50,000 a pair. Do any of you have an extra $50,000 in your pocket?" They usually say, "No." I say, "Do you think I have $50,000 in my pocket? Do your parents have an extra $50,000 in their pockets? So how do you think I paid for these hands?" I get lots of answers like "Because you flew airplanes. Because you have a service dog." I say, "I have these hands because I've got good medical insurance. If I didn't have good medical insurance, I wouldn't have these hands today. But how did I get the good medical insurance?" I get all kinds of answers, and I say, "I got it because I had a good job that gave me good benefits, including medical insurance. But how did I get that good job? Because I went to school. I went to high school and college, and I got a good education. The good education got me the good job, and the good job got me good insurance. If I had not gone to school, I would not have these hands today." So I say to them, "Go to school. Promise me today that you're going to go to high school. And promise me today that you're going to go to college. If you just walk

175

into the classroom and sit down, you'll be surprised at how easy school can be." The teachers all smile when I give that little pep talk.

I feel comfortable with the kids, and I was amazed how easy it was to talk to them. The "hands on" portion of A Touch of Understanding now has several volunteers who have been cross-trained to handle any volunteer requirements. I am joined in the speaking segment by three other people with physical disabilities who discuss their personal situations. In addition to offering my perspective of life as an upper bilateral amputee, I'm pleased that a lower bilateral and an upper unilateral amputee also participate and describe their experiences. Volunteers talk about Parkinson's disease, spinal injuries, head trauma, blindness, autism, and a host of other disabling conditions.

One of our volunteers named Kirsten is autistic and she speaks real low, slow with a calm voice and good enunciation. Part of her speech is "I've never had friends. I always wanted to have friends. I used to pray every night that I'd have friends. Then one day I found out about CCI (Canine Companions for Independence) and they gave me a dog, and I've always had a friend since that day. Now I'm not the little girl with autism in school, I'm the little girl in school with the neat dog. Everybody wants to come pet the dog. Kristen is now attending junior college and giving her time to A Touch of Understanding whenever she can to help children understand what it's like to be autistic.

Another volunteer, Amanda, is 23 years old and she was diagnosed with autism at 5 years of age. She grew up with social workers to help her learn how to play with kids, and she's got a photographic memory. She can open a book, skim a page and tell you every word it says on that page. She likes Disney movies and theatrical productions, and when she's finished with her presentation, I'll say, "Amanda, are you going to do a play for us today?" And she blushes and says, "If you want me to. Which one do you want me to do?" I'll say, "I don't know, *Lion King,* or **Pirates of the Caribbean**?" and she'll recite a whole scene from a play or movie, word-for-word. And she modulates her voice for the different characters. She just amazes me.

We've had so many speakers come through A Touch of Understanding and they feel so good about being able to talk about their disabilities and being able to make a difference for disabled people in an able-bodied world. They have a job to do, and you can just see how much they smile when they get up there and talk. It helps disabled people so much to be able to express themselves as much as it helps the able-bodied people to gain understanding about them.

We receive a lot of favorable comments from teachers and students in days following our presentations. Through the years, teachers have told us about kids whose attitudes changed dramatically after our session. Some of the kids who never spoke about their disabilities or ways in which they differ from their peers now talk about them. I vividly remember meeting one child who underwent numerous complex operations on his legs to straighten them out. When I returned to his school the following year, he came up to me and said, "Remember me? You talked to us, and I got my legs fixed." The teacher told me that the child talks about it all of the time now.

Most of our sessions involve third-grade students or older, but in one memorable presentation I spoke to a group of second graders at a school near Emeryville, California. This little kid in the back room had her hand waving insistently in the air for a question. The teacher said, "pick on Mary." I said, "Yes, Mary?" She asked, "Uh, uh, uh, did the watch come with your hand?" I had to stop and laugh at that one. But that's a second-grade question. Older kids will ask questions like, "How do you take a shower, or how do you comb your hair? How do you brush your teeth?" I'll say, "Just like you do." They'll ask, "Can you write?" I say, "Not as good as you can. I use a computer for everything."

A Touch of Understanding was originally designed to be presented to elementary school children; however, we have expanded to high schools, businesses, civic organizations, and church groups. It is not uncommon for us to make in excess of 100 presentations to as many as 4,000 children and adults a year.

I call my prosthetic hands "tools." Now everyone in our group calls adaptive devices tools. I picked up that term from flying firebombers in Columbia, California. My good friend and pilot Walt Johnson would always say, "I have to go out and wash my tool." An airplane was his tool for making money. He'd say he had to put oil in his tool, or grease his tool. Thus, my hands are simply tools.

When I'm giving my talks, I'm very aware that the kids' attention is focused on my hands. So sometimes in the middle of a sentence I begin rotating my hand. Then I'll look down at it, slap my hand, saying, "Stop that! Bad hand!" That always sparks a giggle, or two.

179

I've learned that one of the biggest handicaps of a disabled person is that able-bodied people put limitations on us. That's for two reasons—first of all, the able-bodied person is uninformed and doesn't understand how limitations can be overcome. We take our world to the children because if there's not a disabled child in the classroom or in the family, they have very little knowledge of our world. They haven't experienced limitations like we have, and they don't think about it, or maybe don't want to think about it. Secondly, they don't think the disabled person has figured out ways to cope with challenges that might not have occurred to them. Consider the fact that in one sense, humans have disabilities with respect to other creatures. For example, we can't fly like birds can. That's a limitation we have—we're stuck on the ground. Whales can swim for hundreds of miles—we can't. So in a sense, we have disabilities compared to other creatures.

Our Touch of Understanding volunteers are wonderful people. Darlene is amazing. Her retinas began to detach when she was in high school. She lost most of her vision in one eye in high school, then at about 35, as a mother of two, she lost vision in the other eye. Her kids were probably 4 or 5 when Darlene lost her sight, but she has found ways to manage her life and to continue to care for her kids.

We also have a presenter named Mike, who fell off a carport as a college senior and sustained a severe closed-head injury. He's in a wheelchair and speaks using a synthesizer. He returned to college after his fall and finished his studies, earning a degree in history. He and his mother do the presentations together using sign language to communicate with each other. Their message for kids is to always wear a helmet when riding a skateboard or bicycle. Another guy named Dan lost both lower legs due to a combination of diabetes and toxic shock syndrome. He now walks as well as we do using two prosthetic legs. He's a recent father, and he travels to developing countries delivering hundreds of wheelchairs each year.

Pam suffers from Parkinson's disease and still rides her horse each week and represents Northern California at national Parkinson's conventions. Patty lost a hand in a childhood accident and competes in cycling, golf, snow skiing and kayaking.

Nancy, an archeologist by profession, has epilepsy. She speaks about service dogs. I first met Nancy at a disability fair in Sacramento, and she had a Canine Companions for Independence (CCI) booth next to our Touch of Understanding booth. I asked if I could talk to her dog, Union, a three-quarter golden retriever and one-quarter black lab mix. She said, "Sure, but tell me about your hands. I want to know about those because I have a cousin who knows a friend who has no hands." She continued, "He lives in Vallejo, and he used to fly airplanes, and he lost his hands in a car accident." I said, "I don't live in Vallejo, I live in Vacaville. I didn't used to fly airplanes—I still fly airplanes, and I lost my hands in a car accident, actually a race car on the Bonneville Salt Flats." Nancy's eyes got as big as donuts, her jaw dropped and she asked in amazement, "Are you him?" I said, "I probably am." She said, "Leonard is my cousin." I said, "Leonard is my best friend and race car partner." Nancy and I became best of friends, and she began speaking about service dogs at Touch of Understanding programs.

I've always had a soft spot for dogs, big golden dogs. In the early '80s, golden Captain came into my life. It was the beginning of a life change for me. I still remember driving to the kennel in Napa, California, and picking up a little bundle of golden fur. I had no idea how he would change my life. A big guy, sometimes his intelligence almost scared me, and for the next 15 years, he was my buddy. Finally on my birthday in 1998 he died in my arms at the age of 15—a loss I'll never forget.

Captain had become a family member, and Mary Ann and I took his loss very hard. Mary Ann said, "No more dogs!" The next couple of years' life without a golden retriever became difficult for me, but Mary Ann still said, "No dogs!" Neither of us realized that another golden retriever, a "special" golden, was waiting to adopt us.

One day Nancy said to me, "Mike, you need one of these CCI dogs," and she invited me and Mary Ann to a CCI open house. The national headquarters of CCI are located in Santa Rosa. With beautifully manicured lawns, dormitory rooms, kennels, veterinary facilities, classrooms and indoor-outdoor training areas, it was an impressive facility. This was my first chance to observe service animals at work, and I was amazed at what these dogs were doing. They were incredible, and it was almost magical the way they assisted their disabled handlers. When not assigned a task the dogs would sit relaxed, ignoring all other people and dogs, waiting for their next command.

I thought to myself, "These dogs are fantastic, and those people really need them." My disability became very minor, in no way could I take one of these fantastic dogs from someone who really needed them. I spoke with the leader of the Santa Rosa program. I said, "I am disabled but I'm pretty capable, so I could never take one of these dogs from someone who really needs one. But how can I get a flunky dog?" A very stern look came upon Troy's face and he said, "We don't have 'flunky' dogs. We have 'change of career' dogs." So I asked, "Oops! How do I get a 'change of career' dog?" He said, "It's usually about a year's wait because they're really in demand." Overhearing the conversation, Nancy sensed my frustration, tapped me on the shoulder and whispered, "Be patient, Mike, I'll work on it."

Service dogs go through a two-three year training program. It begins with a "puppy raiser" and progresses to advanced training and, finally, team training. Initially a puppy raiser is presented with an 8-week-old puppy and spends the next year, or so, teaching the puppy basic commands and to be a good citizen. The puppy raiser is expected to take the puppy everywhere he or she goes and can legally do so because the puppy is classified as a service-dog-in-training. During this time, the pair are required to attend a formal monthly class to evaluate both the puppy's progress and the puppy raiser's technique. It's a sad day when the puppy raiser turns the dog in to CCI for advanced training—their reward is another 8-week-old bundle of fur to train.

During several weeks of advanced training at the CCI campus the dog matures as it is taught more service tasks pertaining to service work. Finally, team training begins. This is when the dog meets the person it will spend its working career with. Team training takes two weeks—14 straight days of classes. It's training for both—the handler learns the proper care of the dog and what to expect, and the dog learns specific tasks to assist its disabled handler. During this time, the recipient lives with his or her dog in the facility's dorm rooms. At the end of team training, the dog graduates and the puppy raiser sees the dog for the final time as he or she formally presents the graduate dog to its recipient—a very emotional event for the puppy raiser.

Puppy raisers are incredible, as I would soon find out. Just think, these pups have become a constant companion, at school and work—everywhere you go. Carly Newbill-Fermer is one such puppy raiser. As a college student, Carly raised Magy, her first puppy. Since then, she has become a senior trainer for CCI Northern California and has many puppies to her credit. She is responsible for initially molding Magy into the lady she is today.

Nancy urged me to visit Steve Forsty's Custom Dog Training School in Roseville, California. She had told me that 75 percent of the dogs flunk, and the puppy raiser has the first choice about what happens to that dog. So I started going to puppy class once a month and began receiving the CCI newsletter. That's where I saw a notice that a dog named Blair had been released at about 10 months old. I immediately called and scheduled an appointment to meet Blair. She was a beautiful, slightly built golden retriever and, against Mary Ann's wishes, I brought Blair home for a "test run."

A test run is usually a two-week period with no commitments to see how the dog fits into your environment. After a couple of days, I called Nancy and said, "I've got Blair," and she said, "No! You didn't get Blair!" I said, "It's only for a test run." She said, "Take Blair back!" Blair was a beautiful dog, but when they release a dog at 10 months, it's usually because it has some undesirable traits. I soon discovered that Blair would have made someone an excellent pet, but she didn't have the drive to do service work.

Mary Ann and I were going on vacation, so we returned Blair and told her raisers we would think about it while on vacation. When we returned, I called the owners and told them we had thought about it, and it just wasn't going to work out. I spoke with Nancy soon after and told her we had taken Blair back, and she said, "Good. I've got Magy for you."

I said, "Tell me about Magy." She said, "She's a golden retriever-yellow lab mix and she's been through the entire program, but she suffers separation anxiety. When she's put in a crate, she chews her feet excessively, an unacceptable trait for a graduate CCI service dog." So I went to puppy school that following week to meet Magy, and four women there wanted to give me their dogs. It was like they were trying to give me their daughters. Suddenly, I had more decisions to make than I could handle. But Nancy said, "Magy would be a great dog for you." So I went over and talked to her. She had gone through puppy training, advanced training, and she was in team training (the final phase) when they discovered she chewed on her feet.

I wanted Magy, but I still had to convince Mary Ann. So we went over to Carly's house and Magy demonstrated all she could do—open doors, sit and stay on command—and Mary Ann finally said, "Okay. We'll take her for a test run." So we brought her home. It was summertime, and the sliding glass door was open. Almost immediately, Magy grabbed one of Captain's tennis balls, trotted outside and leaped into the swimming pool. My raft was sitting on the side of the pool, and she climbed out of the pool, pulled the raft into the water and got on top of it. That evening when we went to bed, Magy jumped up on the bed. Mary Ann said, "Down," and Magy lay down on the bed. We learned that the command Mary Ann should have used was "Off." Magy was doing exactly as Carly had taught her—"down" means to lie down. We realized we had to learn the service dog vocabulary.

So Magy came to live with us in the fall of 1999, and she's been with us ever since. When she's with me, she's a service animal. If she were with anyone else, she would be considered a pet. When she's with me, she can go into restaurants, hotels, and even with me in the passenger compartments of commercial airliners.

Kids in our Touch of Understanding classes always ask me what Magy can do. I tell them she will get newspapers for me and she'll carry my keys, but most of all she gives me tremendous happiness and companionship. We jog together, we go to the gym together. Everywhere I go, she goes. She teaches kids about service animals. I tell the kids that they should never distract a service dog who is on duty. I tell them, "If you want to pet the dog, always ask first."

I often say, "A Touch of Understanding bridges the gap where teachers and parents have a lack of understanding of our disabled world." I don't mean for this to be a derogatory statement, but simply a statement saying that unless there is a disabled person in the classroom or at home, the teachers or parents have little experience dealing with disability awareness.

I have to mention a couple of experiences with kids that I will always remember: Amanda was an 11-year-old blind girl and luckily we had Darlene, a blind volunteer, working with us that day. Darlene has a special way with kids and walked over to speak with Amanda. I asked her teachers if they thought Amanda might like to pet Magy. "Oh, no," was their reply. "Amanda is deathly afraid of dogs!" I whispered to Darlene, "See what you think. If you think it's OK, nod your head, and I'll bring Magy over." Sure enough, we got the head nod. I approached

Amanda and put my prosthetic hand out to shake her hand. As soon as she felt my hand she pulled her hand away and exclaimed, "What is that!" I calmly explained I didn't have any hands and these were prosthetic or mechanical hands. Before she could react, I said to her, "With your hands you can do things I can't." She had a look of amazement as I said, "You can touch and feel things!" I told her my daughter was here, and people often said she had smooth fine hair that was soft to the touch, but I had never felt her hair. Amanda smiled, so I guided her hand to Magy's back. She hesitated asking, "What is this?" I replied, "This is Magy. I call her my daughter. She's actually my best friend, and she goes everywhere with me. Isn't she soft?" Amanda relaxed instantly and a smile came across her face. She said, "You mean she's a dog." I answered, "Yep, she is. Isn't her fur soft and smooth?"

Dogs have a way with kids, and kids have a way with dogs. To everyone's surprise, Amanda continued to pet Magy. She even giggled when Magy wrapped her tongue around her hand. I chuckled to myself…just give her a chance.

Several minutes later, when we had to leave, Amanda asked if she could pet Magy good-bye. I glanced at her teachers. They could not believe what they had just seen.

At our annual Touch of Understanding picnic, a young girl named Courtney was playing Frisbee with her father. I didn't realize it at the time, but her mother was one of our Touch of Understanding officers. Magy looked at me with those big brown eyes that said, "Dad—a Frisbee…I gotta' go play." So we walked over to Courtney, and I asked her if Magy could play Frisbee with her. I removed Magy's cape and she became a real Frisbee dog. Soon, her dad joined her mom on the park bench and they both watched their daughter play with Magy. I watched for a while, then asked her if she would like to see what Magy could do. After a quick lesson, Courtney had Magy responding to a few simple commands, such as *sit, down, roll, heel, side,* and *stay* when she threw the Frisbee. What a team! I went to talk to her mom and dad as she continued to play. I was surprised to learn that Courtney had a minor disability having to do with balance and that she would be eligible to have her own CCI dog. I then explained a little about service dogs and what CCI was all about. I told them there was usually a long wait to get a service dog, but that completing a formal application plus an interview would get things rolling. I am happy to say Courtney now has her own service dog as her best friend.

Talking about my own disabilities is wonderful therapy but it wasn't long before I started to see how it benefits the kids, as well. Since we like to present Touch of Understanding to third- or fourth-grade classes each year, often a sixth-grade students will see us at their school and remember us from the past. A warm "hello," saying "I remember you from a couple years ago," is always a special reward for me.

I can say that life with a service animal is absolutely incredible. Your quality of life becomes so much better. Magy is an icebreaker for me—the center of attraction and an ambassador of goodwill—wherever we go. We often walk through the shopping mall and always observe leash laws. The funny part is that Magy usually carries her own leash. We educate people about our world—the disabled world—and introduce them to service animals. We have fun everywhere we go together. A dog's love is unconditional, and I believe my life gets better every day because Magy is a part of it.

Chapter 14

Trading Airplanes for Agility

I was flipping channels on the TV one day and landed on dog agility competitions airing on the Discovery Channel's *Animal Planet* series. I thought, "This looks like a lot of fun!" I was wrapped up in the Touch of Understanding program and just enjoying having Magy, but I thought, "That would be a good activity for Mary Ann and Magy to do together." I called Mary Ann into the family room and said, "Come and look at this agility training. Do you think you'd like to do this with Magy?" She watched for a few minutes and said, "No."

I said to her, "I'm going to take an agility lesson and find out what it's all about. Will you think about it?" and she replied, "No. I don't want to do it, but it sounds like something you might enjoy."

I was already in the process of taking Magy to obedience school at Franchesca's Dog Training outside of Dixon, California. Because I was interested in agility, I asked her if she knew where I could take some agility training. She said, "My friend Marna Obermiller is an excellent agility instructor. She calls her school 'precision chaos' and she's also right here in Dixon. In contacting Marna, she said, "We have a beginner's class, but it's about halfway through." I asked her if we could come visit and she could give me and Magy a practical evaluation for agility training. She agreed, so I took Magy through her obedience paces and Marna told us we could start the following Saturday.

A fairly new sport, dog agility first began in England in the late 1970s to serve as entertainment during the breaks at horse-jumping competitions. Since then, it has evolved into a popular and exciting international event. It's a competitive sport that tests a person's skills in training and handling of dogs over a timed obstacle course. Competitors direct their dogs to jump hurdles, scale ramps, pass through tunnels, navigate a teeter totter and weave through a line of poles. Agility scores reflect speed and accuracy while maneuvering around obstacles.

Any dog with good physical condition and energy can compete in the sport. The American Kennel Club (AKC) has identified more than 200 breeds of dogs (including mixed-breeds as a single group) that have demonstrated their ability to perform well. An agility trial encompasses a series of skills and obstacles:

- Dog walk
- Open tunnel
- Teeter-totter
- Closed tunnel (chute)
- A-frame
- Tire jump
- Bar jumps
- Weave poles

There are several agility organizations, and although we competed and titled in all of them, our main concentration was on Canine Performance Events (CPE). CPE has five levels of difficulty. They are defined by 1-5 and championship. Championship, which is the ultimate program, is unique because it requires approximately 230 clean runs to attain a C-ATE (CPE-Agility Team Extraordinaire) championship.

For our first agility lesson, Marna had set up two very simple jumps and a table. She placed guides to form a channel so Magy would be forced to go through the channel and over the jumps to get to the table. When we were ready, Marna said, "I'll hold Magy here and you go over by the table and call her. When she sees you, I'll release her." But when I called Magy, I think she cleared both jumps at once, hit the table going about 30 miles an hour and knocked me down. Her training up to that point had been pretty much indoors or restricted by a leash and commands. Outdoors, on the grass, and off-leash seemed to be a new and exciting world for her. We

Mike and Magy at an agility competition in Dixon, CA
(Photo by Jeff March)

tried the same maneuver a few more times that day, and finally got it down pretty well.

The next exercise included a tire hanging on a frame, and Magy's challenge was to jump through the center of it. Beyond the tire was a tunnel. When we were ready, I called Magy, she jumped through the tire, ran through the tunnel like a bat out of hell, almost knocked me down again, found a toy and off she went. At that point, Marna said, "Mike, why don't you and Magy go over there and practice some obedience training."

Our first lesson was fairly unsuccessful, but I wasn't ready to give up on it. Our next couple of lessons were a bit better, but Marna could detect the frustration I was experiencing. All of the other dog handlers were using treats, which are important tools for training, but my lack of hands prevented me from giving Magy treats. Marna came up with the idea of using a chopped-up hot dog. She put a piece of hot dog in her mouth and spit it at Magy. At that point, Magy would do anything for a hot dog. Marna put her through some basic obedience maneuvers, and Magy did a great job because the treats became motivation. As soon as I started spitting hot dog pieces at her, Magy was like a brand new dog. When the dog is looking at the handler, he/she has complete control. When the dog is looking off into who knows where, the handler has no control. So I used hot dogs that entire lesson and we made tremendous progress. We finished our training and went home around lunch time to find Mary Ann fixing—of all things—hot dogs!

Magy and I attended agility training classes once and sometimes twice a week for almost two years before Marna told us we were ready to compete. Because of Marna's thorough training, we were more than ready for agility competitions. We could do all of the difficult maneuvers because we had very solid building blocks of learning. At home, I had two jumps and weave poles for practice. I did some extra training with the teeter-totter by putting a 1-foot by 10-foot board flat on the ground

Mike with Magy pole weaving (Photo by Jeff March)

to get Magy used to walking across it. When I finally placed the teeter-totter on the fulcrum at the lowest setting, she had no problems crossing it. I bought a set of weave poles from Marna and first arranged them so they were flat. After what seemed like several hundred times through them, slowly I would lift up poles six inches, and we'd try that about a hundred times. As I raised the poles gradually, Magy was forced to snake through them. Eventually, I lifted the poles until they were vertical, and Magy could weave though them on her own. People use several different methods for teaching a dog how to weave through the poles, which is one of the hardest things to learn. We worked on it several times a day for a month before Magy could finally weave. In only four weeks she was able to do 12 weave polls.

Body language is very important in agility. I can take Magy through an agility course without saying a word, because she can read my body language. She looks to see which way my feet are pointing, how my shoulders are placed, whether my arm is up or down, and in which direction I'm looking. They also claim that hand signals are very important, but I proved them wrong.

The four main agility organizations are CPE (Canine Performance Events, www.k9cpe.com); AKC (American Kennel Club, www.akc.org/events/agility); USDAA (U.S.

Mike and Magy competing

Dog Agility Association, www.usdaa.com); and NADAC (North American Dog Agility Council, www.nadac.com).

Our first competition was a CPE-sponsored competition in Elk Grove, California. CPE headquarters is based in South Lyons, Michigan. Magy and I competed at Level 1, which doesn't require any weaves or the teeter totter. It's designed to motivate the handler to go on to the next level. A Level-2 competition includes six weaves and a teeter totter. Level-3 competition includes all 12 weaves and the teeter totter. So it's progressive learning.

In June 2005, Magy and I were part of an eight-person, 15-dog caravan. We drove 2,000 miles to CPE nationals in Fowlerville, Michigan, and I was the only guy with seven women, who all had dogs competing in the agility trials. Needless to say, they treated me well but made sure I was able to toe the line.

In Michigan Magy and I were at level 5 and we qualified on 6 of 9 runs. The runs are timed and you have to make time on the runs with few faults. The course configuration is always different. You learn the layout from a course map the day of the competition. The handler and dog have never practiced on that particular course. In the end, the trip was a lot of fun, but exhausting.

CPE has five levels of competition, and you earn titles at each level. It took us about two years to advance from Level 1 to Level 5. After completing Level 5, CPE has a category called the C-ATCH (CPE-Agility Trial Champion) Championship. Magy qualified for C-ATCH in July 2005, and she was the 126th dog in the nation to earn her C-ATCH designation.

Our next goal was to make the C-ATE level (CPE-Agility Team Extraordinaire) or the highest level in CPE competition. In 2005, only three dogs in the nation were at the C-ATE level. Dogs can compete in the veterans status at six years of age, but they can compete as long as they're fit and able.

Mike and Magy competing

Some breeds excel much faster in agility trials, for example, border collies are absolutely phenomenal because they have drive, they want to please their handler and they're fast. Australian shepherds are great, then labs and goldens. The AKC organization requires pedigree dogs to compete, but Magy qualifies in a category called IPL (individual privileged listing), which means she's accepted as a golden retriever through her looks and traits, even though she doesn't have papers. The other organizations don't require the dogs to have a pedigree.

In 2005, we completed 30 weekend competitions. The competitions are either outdoors or in a covered arena—like a horse arena with no sides.

The agility people all know me, and they're my family. After my friend and adopted dad Ted Heineman died in 2005, Magy and I attended his memorial service in Southern California. It was the same weekend as an agility trial in Turlock, so we went to the memorial service on Saturday and drove up to the agility competition in Turlock on Sunday. When I arrived, my agility friends said, "Where were you yesterday? We were worried about you. Don't do this again, or tell us if you're not going to be here." It was a good feeling knowing they had worried about me, and that's when I knew for sure we were family.

When I first started in the agility sport, people didn't know how I could do agility without hands. I remember a run in Elk Grove in the rain. Magy loves mud and she had been playing in it then she jumped on me and her teeth accidentally bumped my stump, causing it to bleed—they bleed real easily. So Magy and I were covered in mud and my stump was bleeding and when it was our turn to take the start line, the judge looked at us and said, "Are Lady and the pirate ready?" So we had a good run. I was out of breath and sat down on a bale of hay and this lady came over to me and said, "We've never seen a service dog in agility." I said, "This isn't a service dog." She said, "Well, she appears to be a service dog." At that point, Magy put her head in my lap, and the lady smiled and said, "Yep. She's a service dog." I said, "Yeah, you guessed it and she's my best friend and my shadow." The lady asked if she could pet Magy (always ask before petting a service dog), and with a smile she said, "You two are quite a team."

It was muddy and miserable that winter day with puddles you could sail a battleship in. Magy was out there playing in a mud puddle and these three ladies walked by with their fluffy white dogs, and pretty soon all three dogs were playing in the mud puddle with Magy. It seems as if dogs have a special communications ability for things like that. I then heard the ladies yelling, "Trixie, Pixie… come here. Look how dirty you are."

In May of 2007, Magy finally earned the highest level in competition—CPE–Agility Team Extraordinaire (C-ATE). We continued to compete in 30 trials throughout 2008, and retired from competition in December of that year. We had a very successful six-year run, competing in nearly 100 trials. Magy was an amazing competitor and I couldn't have asked for a better companion. A wall in my house displays Magy's accomplishments, including 2002

Therapy Dogs Inc. Pet Therapy Team, 2003 AKC Canine Good Citizen, 2004 AKC Excellent Agility Jumper, 2005 CPE CATCH, 2007 CPE C-ATE, and 2012 AKC Therapy Dog Title Certificate.

Mary Ann and I got Joyce, another golden retriever, in 2007 from Assistance Dogs International (ADI) in Santa Rosa, California (http://www.assistancedogsinternational. org.) While Joyce is a wonderful companion to us and Magy, she didn't quite have what it takes to be an agility competitor. I've thought about getting another dog and re-entering the competition but, as I get older, getting up at 4:30 a.m. to attend all-day events isn't quite as appealing as it used to be.

These days, Mary Ann, Magy, Joyce and I are enjoying our retirement by spending several months a year traveling around the Western United States in a motor home.

Magy and Joyce swimming in Colter Bay at Grand Teton National Park

Chapter 15

Epilogue

Looking back on my life, I realize that I've had the opportunity to experience a lot of things many people would never even attempt—flying airplanes, landing on an aircraft carrier, supersonic flight in a single engine aircraft, extinguishing forest fires from the air, driving race cars, becoming a captain for a commercial airline, building and flying aerobatic airplanes, winning air races and aerobatic contests, competing in dog agility competitions, and teaching children acceptance of people with disabilities. All of these things have shaped who I am today.

The hardest adjustment I had to make after losing my hands was to focus on what I *can* do rather than dwelling on what I *cannot* do. Yes, I underwent a lot of internal emotional struggles and intense depression during the first couple of years of recovery. I might not have pushed on without the unwavering support of Mary Ann and some very close friends who stood by me and encouraged me. As I began emerging from the darkness, I completed a personal inventory and found that my capabilities outweighed my incapacities. That's when I recognized that my destiny was still within my grasp. The stubbornness that had defined much of my life was still intact—to my advantage. I knew I could never build airplanes again, but I was sure that I could hold the stick of an airplane and fly it. That burning desire to fly, as well as the conviction to never take "no" for an answer, got me through the worst of my ordeal. In my Touch of Understanding talks, I always tell the kids, "Don't worry about what you don't have, be thankful for what you do have."

My return to the cockpit was hard-fought, and perhaps the most gratifying accomplishment of my life. I no longer fly airplanes, though, because I have developed newer interests. I'm having the time of my life discovering the magnificent national treasures the United States has to offer. In 2005, Mary Ann and I bought our first recreational vehicle (RV) with a friend of ours and started taking short trips around California. It was a little 23-foot motor home (I call a shoebox), and the main reason we bought it was to be able to take trips with our dogs Magy and Joyce, and our rescued golden retriever, Taylor, whom we had for too short a time. Our first outing was to the gold discovery town of Coloma on the American River. We took several short trips to Plumas National Forest, Morro Bay, and Cayucos on the California coast. Years ago, we had found Cayucos to be a really dog-friendly place when we stayed in a hotel there. The hotel room doors had peep-holes for humans and peep-holes for dogs, and they had a dog wash in back. But not too many hotels are as welcoming to dogs and their owners.

In 2007 we bought a 31-foot Tiffin Allegro motor home and ventured in and out of California. We always try to go after the snow stops and before school gets out (a very narrow window), because it's not as crowded in the campgrounds. Since then, we have visited Yellowstone National Park twice, and all of the national parks in Utah. In 2012, we spent 70 days on the road, traveling around the country enjoying the state and national parks. During our second stay at Yellowstone, we experienced what the park was like during a heavy snowfall—in May. We were advised to move from the campground into the town of West Yellowstone, and we're glad we did because the RV heater broke, and we had to purchase space heaters to stay warm. I'll never forget Magy making snow angels in the fresh white snow. That year, we also visited Cody, Wyoming, Grand Teton National Park, Glacier National Park, and Death Valley.

We toured Hoover Dam (once known as Boulder Dam) and Lake Mead. The new highway bridge over the Colorado River in Black Canyon south of the dam is phenomenal. You can't see anything from the roadway on the bridge because of high walls that were built to prevent drivers from gawking. Hoover Dam really redefines huge. It's 720 feet high, and it's holding back a lake that extends for 100 miles. We took two tours of the dam – the upper tour and the bottom tour. One of the dam's enormous flood control release gates can drain 78,000 gallons of water per second from the lake into the river downstream.

One of our favorite California stops was the Lone Pine Film History Museum, on U.S. 395. Nearly 300 motion pictures made between the 1920s and '50s, including dozens of western movies, contained footage that was filmed between Lone Pine and Mt. Whitney. We took our little tow car on a dirt road where all these movies had been filmed. You can buy a self-tour map, set your odometer to zero and go down the old movie road for a set number of miles on the map and see all the major film sets for old movies. For example, drive three-tenths of a mile, look straight ahead, and that's where they filmed *Gunga Din*. It took place in India, but very few people notice Mt. Whitney in the background. We saw a western movie called *Django Unchained*, directed by Quentin Tarantino and filmed in 2012. I think I noticed Mt. Whitney in the background, so we figured they must still occasionally use that area for movie sets.

Mary Ann and I are getting a great historical view of the United States in our travels, and it's such an enjoyable way to spend time with our friends and dogs. We've met a lot of nice people in our journeys, and are planning to keep it up as long as we're able.

Where would I be today if life hadn't thrown me that traumatic twist of fate? Most likely I would have become a retired airline captain with lots of toys and plenty of money, but none of the compassion I have developed for people, animals and kids.

I've got to say that Mary Ann is the best thing that ever happened to me, and without her I know my life would have taken a completely different, possibly less accomplished path.

As they say, "life is good!"

The Authors

Mike Penketh poses with his best friend Magy (Frisbee hanging from her tooth), and co-authors Marti Smiley Childs and Jeff March of EditPros LLC in Davis, CA. For more information, visit www. editpros.com on the Web (photo by Amanda Domingues)

Amputee Resources

Hanger Prosthetics & Orthotics Inc. was established by 18-year-old engineering student James Edward Hanger, who left college in 1861 to serve in the Confederate Army. On June 3, less than two days after enlisting, a cannonball tore through his leg early in the Battle of Philippi. After becoming the first amputee of the Civil War, Hanger whittled from barrel staves the first "Hanger limb," and in 1891 he was granted a U.S. patent for his prosthetic innovation.

Hanger Prosthetics has more than 700 patient care clinics throughout the United States. The company's website has an excellent list of links to peer support resources, including books, publications and organizations for amputees at **http://www.hanger.com/prosthetics/experience/pages/peersupport.aspx**

Stumps 'R Us is a non-profit organization, started by Dan Sorkin (DanSorkin@gmail.com), a radio personality for more than 50 years in Chicago and San Francisco, and a pilot and flight instructor. Dan lost his leg in a motorcycle accident, and established Sumps 'R Us to bring together amputees and their loved ones to learn from each other, exchange information, explore ongoing state-of-the-art technology and share growth, humor, and personal experiences. Dan's website **http://www.stumps.org** also has a comprehensive list of links for amputees and their families.

CPSIA information can be obtained at www.ICGtesting.com
Printed in the USA
BVOW010559300413

319425BV00007B/16/P